OUT OF THE FIRE
& Into the Light

OUT OF THE FIRE
& Into the Light

A revealing story of abuse, betrayal and healing

LORI FRISCH

WITH RITA BRHEL

iUniverse, Inc.
Bloomington

Out of the Fire & Into the Light

iUniverse books may be ordered through booksellers or by contacting:

iUniverse
1663 Liberty Drive
Bloomington, IN 47403
www.iuniverse.com
1-800-Authors (1-800-288-4677)

ISBN: 978-1-4620-4922-6 (sc)
ISBN: 978-1-4620-4923-3 (ebk)

Printed in the United States of America

iUniverse rev. date: 09/13/2011

CONTENTS

Acknowledgments

God sent people to help me when I needed them the most.
I cannot thank Julie Lang, Krista Lang, and Whitney Daberkow enough
for giving up their time to see this project through.
I thank God for assembling these gifted and talented ladies to help me
tell this story.
Each of you is such a blessing to me.

Dedications

To my boys,
I've made mistakes along the way, but I have always acted out of love.
Sometimes I have to smile and think I did a few things right, because
look at the wonderful men that you have become. I'm so proud of you
both! Thank you for supporting me and refreshing my memory through
this painful process.

To my wonderful husband Glenn,
Who cries with me whenever I tell this story, sharing in my pain as well
as in my joy.
I love you so much!

To Amy Hughes,
Who helped me find my way back to God. I am eternally grateful.

To Tim and Katie,
I couldn't ask for a better family.

To all of my friends and family,
I am truly blessed by having each one of you in my life!

Authors Note

I live by this rule: Is this going to matter five years from now? Most of the time the answer is no, but there are other times when it most definitely does matter.

I originally wrote this biography for my sons to help them understand the decisions that I made. But this story has become much more. Putting it down on paper has brought me incredible healing, and as God never wastes a hurt, it has also helped many others. God has opened to me a prison ministry to female inmates. This story has been sent to them to offer encouragement. I receive letters daily of how my story has been used to touch these women, and offer hope. It is my desire to reach farther with that hope. I have learned that one cannot deal with the past by escaping it. I have confronted and overcome my deepest fears.

I once heard a preacher say, "If you don't deal with the past, the past will continue to deal with you." Truer words were never spoken.

Another wise man told me that, in order to tell an effective story, one must cut her heart open and write about whatever spills out. If all of the pain and sorrow that I have been through can be used to help someone else, then it would not have been in vain. Some of the names have been changed, as this book was not written to embarrass or hurt anyone, but rather to give hope.

Lori Frisch

On my eighteenth birthday, I saw a check lying on the kitchen table. It was my father's final child support payment.
Scrawled in the memo were the words, "finally free!"
Is that all I was to you . . . a burden?
I felt like I was being discarded . . .

ONE

Longing to be Daddy's Girl

*"For I know the plans that I have for you," declares the Lord,
"plans to prosper you and not to harm you, to give you a future
and a hope."*

—Jeremiah 29:11

My mother, a beautiful, intelligent girl with blue eyes and soft brown hair, was named Elaine. Mama came from a middle class family, yet my grandmother strived for upper class society.

My dad, Earl, was just shy of six feet tall, slender, and handsome, with brown hair and hazel eyes. He was the youngest child of five, the surprise baby born after a large gap. He grew up in the pool hall café that his parents owned, learning independence early and practically raising himself, before joining the Navy immediately after high school.

Earl and Elaine married in 1954 despite my grandparents' disapproval. Three years later, they had a daughter, Wendy, who favored my mother in looks. Soon after, they moved to a Naval base in Hawaii.

While in the Navy, my dad served on the *USS Durant*, a radar picket ship. He was often gone. Once when my father's ship had docked, my sister ran up to a bewildered sailor, who happened to be African American, yelling, "Daddy! Daddy!" It is sad to think that Wendy had no idea who her daddy was.

Reflecting back, Mama told me that all was not well with their marriage. When my dad was on board a ship for months at a time, Mama would stay up half the night, every night, writing him a letter. He eventually wrote back, "Please stop writing to me. I don't have time to read your letters!" Any other Navy man would kill for a letter from home, especially from a beautiful, young wife. But Mama stopped writing as my dad requested, sinking deeper into loneliness and depression.

My family moved back to the mainland after a year, and my dad was stationed near Duluth, Minnesota. He decided to leave the Navy and join the Air Force.

I was born in Minnesota three years after my sister, and I favored my father in looks. My given name was Lori, but everyone called me Sister. Mama and Daddy were expecting a boy and were disappointed with another girl. My dad was sent to Greenland soon after I was born. He was later stationed in Thailand, the Philippines, and Viet-Nam.

He seemed to be gone for every birthday and holiday. I always received a souvenir and a currency bill from whatever country he was in at the time. I re-read each letter until they were worn out, tucking them under my pillow to keep him close to me at night. It hurt watching other kids. I was jealous of my friends whose fathers took them places and were home every night. I had no idea what that would be like. They had someone to tuck them in at night; I was lucky to get a letter addressed to me each month. My dad was a stranger to me. *Do you think about me, Daddy, the way that I think about you?*

When I was six, we relocated to a base in Tucson, Arizona. Daddy retired from the Air Force in 1967 and took a job as a Pima County deputy sheriff on the night shift, so once again, I rarely saw him. He worked his way up until he was the head of the identification unit, photographing crime scenes. He was an expert marksman and rode with a posse that searched the desert for missing people. He loved what he did, and I was proud of him.

I remember that Daddy had a "forbidden trunk" in the shed that I was warned to stay out of—which made me want to see its contents even more. Waiting for the opportune moment, I would sneak out to the trunk and peek inside. It was full of black and white photographs of accidents, homicides, and other crime scenes that Daddy had taken at work. They were often quite gruesome to look at, but I was fascinated even so.

One time, my dad had taken some very graphic photographs of a young female hitchhiker. This girl had been brutally beaten and killed, and with young daughters at home, my dad had difficulty handling this case. He showed us the photographs and said, "This is what happens when you take rides with strangers; you will *not* hitchhike, will you?" With wide

eyes, I shook my head. I was too afraid to even contemplate it. My sister on the other hand had already been hitchhiking and saw nothing wrong with it. Thankfully, Wendy never ended up in one of his photographs.

I fought for my father's approval. I tried to be a good daughter by doing what I was told and being respectful. It was worth all the hard work of getting good grades just to get those five seconds of approval from my father, only to go and start all over again. My reward was a dollar bill for every A and a pat on the back for a job well done. I wanted so badly for him to be pleased with me.

Daddy never spanked me or raised his voice. When I would do something that required discipline, he sat me down on my bed and calmly explained what I had done wrong. My life revolved around gaining his approval, and I felt crushed if he was ever displeased with me.

Wendy tried to gain attention in other ways. Every word that came out of her mouth was a lie, and she began to steal. When Wendy was twelve years old, Mama took her to counseling, not knowing what else to do. The therapist asked Wendy, "Why do you lie so much?"

She shrugged her shoulders and nonchalantly replied, "It's the first thing that pops into my head."

After countless run-ins with teachers and store owners, on Wendy's account, Mama had a nervous breakdown. My father's absence while raising two children added to her stress and was probably a major factor in my sister's behavior, also.

My childhood taught me how to adapt to change. I attended eight different schools: five of them, grade schools. I had to make friends quickly, because chances were, we would not be staying long.

Finally, my family settled down and purchased five acres in the hills south of Old Tucson. Each of us had our own horse to ride. Every day, I would take my pony on a new trail. It was so peaceful there, a whole new beginning for us.

One Sunday afternoon when I was ten years old, Wendy was riding her bay horse, Stormy, when Mama called out for her to feed the horses. Wendy instead took Stormy one more turn around the yard. Figuring that their riding session was finished, Stormy slipped into her corral. As they passed the gate, Stormy tried to rub Wendy off, and since she was riding bareback, Wendy pulled her legs up. Stormy then whipped around, and Wendy reached for his mane, spooking the horse. As Wendy fell, she looked up to see the under belly of the horse and a hoof coming down, directly onto her chest.

Mama and I rushed over to Wendy, yelling frantically, "Wendy! Are you hurt? Can you hear me, Wendy?"

She mumbled incoherently. Mama ran to get my grandfather who was visiting at the time. Grandpa yelled, "We should call an ambulance!"

Mama replied, "We can get her to the hospital sooner if we drive her."

"She might die on the way, if we do that," Grandpa said.

Mama ran back to me and said, "You stay with Wendy while I go make the call. Whatever you do, don't let her fall asleep! She could die if she goes to sleep!"

Wendy was so tired. I kept shouting at her while patting her face, "You have to stay awake! Don't fall asleep, Wendy! Mama said you will die if you do!" It seemed to take forever for the ambulance to arrive. *Don't die, Wendy. Please don't die.*

The impact had punctured Wendy's lung and broken her collarbone, putting her in the hospital for two weeks. Wendy was very popular while there. Everyone wanted to see the girl with the imprint of a horseshoe on her chest.

I have a scar the size of a nickel on the back of my thigh, a reminder of my own special day. While in junior high, I was playing softball during a physical education class. As one person would get up to bat, the rest of us would slide down one spot on the old wooden bench. As I slid down, a sliver nearly two inches long went into the back of my thigh. The pain was excruciating. The school nurse called my dad to take me to the doctor. He looked at my wound and decided to remove the shard himself.

He took me home and laid me face down on a hard table. He put his magnifying glasses that he used for leatherworking on his head, and with no anesthesia and using what seemed to be a very dull needle, he began to dig—for what seemed like an hour. I was clutching the edges of the table screaming, "Daddy, Stop it! You're hurting me!" It felt like he was trying to pull all of meat out of my leg through that little hole. Finally, he gave up and took me to the clinic. The doctor numbed the area, had the sliver out in a minute, and rewarded me with a large cherry sucker. Daddy cussed the whole way home, "I can't believe I spent $30 on a stupid sucker."

I felt so inferior to my sister. She was beautiful, had the voice of an angel, and had a natural gift of artistic expression. Everything that she put her mind to, she succeeded in doing. I was awkward, an ugly duckling with uncontrollable hair, and had no talent whatsoever. I was always trying live up to my sister's accomplishments.

But Wendy was also a troubled girl. It's easy to see now that she was screaming to be noticed and loved, but at that time, it seemed that she was

just incorrigible. In reality, she was looking for acceptance in all the wrong ways. Fathers don't realize what an important role they actually play in a young girl's life. When a father is absent, his daughter tends to fill that void with men, drugs, alcohol, or anything else that will make her feel loved.

At the age of twelve, I started making summer visits to my grandparents' home in Kansas. Night after night, I lay in bed on the back porch, far enough out of ear shot—or so they thought. One night, I overheard them say, "Why is that girl so stupid? She is just never going to amount to anything. How can anyone be so dumb?" Sadness consumed me . . . *I wish I was never born.*

If you hear something long enough, you tend to believe the lies. *Maybe they're right. Maybe I am stupid.* Funny, they were so nice to me the next day. But it was hard for me to go on as though nothing had happened, knowing the way that they truly felt about me. Why they agreed to have me come and stay each summer, I don't know.

My grandparents did not believe in hugging or kissing a child; they were to be seen and not heard. Manners were of the upmost importance. "Sit up straight, on the edge of the chair. Don't clink your spoon against  the side of the cup. Stir it quietly like so. Wear your good clothes. We must look proper at all times," Granny said. I felt like I was being groomed to be part of the royal family, but then again, Granny was the president of the toastmistress club and had a reputation to uphold.

On the next visit to my grandparents' house, I overheard Granny say, "How are we going to tell Sister that her folks are getting divorced?"

Divorced? I guess I shouldn't have been shocked. Daddy was gone so much of the time, and Mama was miserable.

"What I can't believe is that she fell in love with another man," Grandpa said.

What? My ears strained to hear their conversation. *What other man?*

"Why, he's just a boy," Granny hissed.

What boy? Who are they talking about?

"They never should have taken that boy into their home," Grandpa scoffed.

Oh my gosh. Mama's in love with Gary? That can't be. Gary was the scrawny, redheaded boy that my sister had run away with when she was fifteen. *How could Mama be in love with him?* He's only seventeen!

Mama picked me up at the airport the following month. "I have something that I need to tell you," she said.

"I know all about it. I heard Granny and Grandpa talking, and I know about Gary, too." Throwing my suitcase down, I grumbled, "How could you do this to Daddy and me?"

"Sister, I haven't felt loved in a very long time, and Gary really loves me."

"Mama, he's five years older than me!"

I stomped off to the car.

"So how was your summer trip?" she replied.

Folding my arms, I let out a huff, "It was good until now."

Mama married Gary when he turned eighteen. She was thirty-eight. The wedding was held at our house, so I went to visit my friend for the day, slamming the door in protest behind me.

When I came home, Mama said, "I was really sad that you didn't come to the wedding."

"Sorry, but I just couldn't bring myself to join in the celebration."

I wasn't the only one: My grandparents wanted to remove Mama from their will.

I didn't speak to my stepfather for three months; we silently passed each other in the hall. I tried to avoid him as much as possible. He and I used to hang around together, but now I felt betrayed by both of them.

At times, he would try to give me orders to do something. *Excuse me?* Someone that was just five years older than me was not going to tell me what to do!

Through the course of my mother's 24-year marriage to Gary, I saw my mom blossom because she was finally loved and I gradually gained respect for Gary. He treated my mother well and honestly loved her.

Mama and Gary had a daughter named Dina. Ten months later, Mama was to have her long-awaited son. I remember the three of us walking down the sidewalk one day. My mother was pregnant with my brother, and so I carried Dina. People were looking at me, like I was the mother and that Gary was with me. I caught their stares and a sense of humiliation engulfed me.

My brother was born on my sixteenth birthday. Gary said to Mama, "I think we should name him Philip after your father." Grandpa beamed with pride when he heard the baby's name and was able to lay aside his distaste for Gary. At the time, I was not terribly thrilled by Philip's arrival.

"This baby is ruining my birthday," I whined. *This is the worst day of my life.*

Granny was in the hospital after a stroke, which had caused my mother to go into labor. I had to babysit Dina, while everyone else was at the hospital. I was a teenager with a social life; I didn't want to be tied down with children. *This was Mama's choice in life, not mine.* Why did I have to get dragged into it?

Earlier that year, Gary lost his job at the lumber yard. I suggested, "Let's move to Kansas to be near Granny and Grandpa."

Gary agreed, "We could have a fresh start on life." Mama sadly packed up her lifetime of possessions into a U-Haul van and headed north.

I needed to finish up a few months of school, so I stayed behind with friends. When it was time for me to leave Tucson, my dad took me to the bus station and I tearfully hugged him and said, "I love you Daddy! I'm really going to miss you."

He patted my back, "Bye Sister. Be a good girl now."

I kept waving as he slowly faded into the distance, and for the next few hours, I sobbed quietly to myself. *What if I never see you again?*

We settled in Deshler, Nebraska, instead of Kansas due to the availability of jobs and housing. Mama and Gary weren't fully prepared for the limited resources in a town of 900, compared with the vastness of Tucson. After that first winter, I don't think Mama ever forgave me. She missed Tucson terribly; she left her lifelong friends and her entire life behind, and now had to start completely over. Gary, however, was eager to start his new life. I missed the warm desert and all of my friends, but I was looking forward to this new adventure.

When we moved to Nebraska, I was in my junior year of high school. The kids I went to school with had known each other since kindergarten, and I was an outsider.

A handsome boy named Steve asked me on a date that first winter. He was as tall as my dad, with broad shoulders, sandy blond hair, and blue eyes. He had the biggest Donny Osmond smile. We were both sixteen.

He was very loyal, and fun to be with. His family was warm and welcoming to me, and I loved all of them. Steve hoped that we would marry after high school. He wanted a career as an engineer for the railroad. His dad worked on the railroad, and was gone all week, home only on the weekend. His mother raised all of the children almost single-handedly. I didn't want the same fate for my life. I wanted a husband who would be home with me every night. I had already lived that life and didn't want a repeat performance. And so, I made the difficult decision to break up with him after two years of dating. It was hard, but I felt that I was making the right decision.

TWO

Mrs. Somebody

For the Lord GOD will help me; therefore I will not be disgraced;
therefore I have set my face like a flint, and I know that I will
not be ashamed.

—Isaiah 50:7

In 1978, I had just turned eighteen and the Thayer County Sheriff's Department hired me as a dispatcher on the graveyard shift. A deputy named Bob came to work there and, in about six months, was staying way past his shift to talk to me.

He helped me fix my broken-down jalopy. Laughter rang out underneath the hood. We started dating after a few months, and he took

me home to meet his family, who farmed corn and soybeans near Geneva, Nebraska. Oh how I wished later that I would have seen the warning signs: His family could not speak to each other civilly. His dad yelled, "Get out if you can't stop yelling! Leave my house now!" Bob and his brother were relentless in criticizing their mom, leaving her in tears much of the time. It grieved me to see how they treated her, especially right in front of a guest.

But Bob didn't treat me that way. Once, I came out to help him prepare the field for planting. I was driving the tractor while he fixed the fence. A post was sticking up in the field, and I hit it with the front axle. Bob was very gracious to me, telling me, "It's going to be fine. We will get it fixed. Don't worry about it." I felt terrible, but he never got upset with me about it. He even laughed about the situation.

He told me disturbing stories of his childhood, "See this scar here," pointing to a gash on his chin, "That's where our pig bit me because I was torturing him. I also held mock trials with my sister's kittens, hanging the guilty ones. It was so funny."

"That's not funny to kill innocent kittens, and I'm sure you deserved whatever the pig did to you," I retorted.

After ten months of dating, I got pregnant. Bob responded, "What on earth were you thinking that you could let this happen?"

I was happy about it and told him, "Everything will work out. It will be fine; you'll see." After much discussion, we decided to get married. He didn't want to get married but agreed that it was the right thing to do.

I had just turned twenty. Thinking back, I was much too young to be getting married, but at that time, I wanted to be Mrs. Somebody. This most likely reverts back to the absent father syndrome and needing to feel a sense of security and belonging.

"Are you sure you know what you're doing, Sister?" Mama said. "Do you even love him?"

"Sure I love him. And we're going to be really happy," I said.

We had a private ceremony on October 3, 1980, with just my mother and the pastor present. I wore a white prom dress that my mother had made for me. During our first few weeks of marriage, Bob was increasingly more agitated about the pregnancy. He was relentless as he harped, "A child is going to ruin our lives. Can't you understand that? We are never going to be able to do anything. Our marriage will be destroyed unless you get rid of it. Do the best thing for us and take care of this problem *now!*"

I was very hurt. *Wasn't this why we got married, to give this child a father and a mother?* After several weeks, I decided that I did not want our marriage to start off with him being so angry at me all the time. Reluctantly, I called a doctor's office in Omaha, Nebraska, that performed abortions.

I was about five weeks into the pregnancy, and I had convinced myself that it was not really a baby at that point. No counseling or ultrasound was ever offered to me, or I likely would have changed my mind. During the two-hour drive to Omaha, Bob reassured me that we were doing the right thing. I was so nervous and scared, wishing that he would change his mind, but he wanted the "problem" gone. He told me that we would go out to celebrate afterward by buying me a new outfit and having dinner. *Like that would somehow make it all better.*

When we arrived, Bob took a seat in the waiting room and assured me, "Everything is going to be fine. You are doing the right thing." As the assistant led me through the door, I gazed back at Bob with a pleading look, to which he waved at me to keep going. There was no turning back.

I was shown to a sterile room that looked just like every other doctor's office. The assisting nurse was pregnant, which added to my shame. I couldn't imagine how a person who was about to give new life could participate in taking one. After I changed into a flimsy gown, the nurse had me lie down on an examination table. With no anesthesia administered, I can remember tremendous pain when they inserted a tube into my womb. I grabbed the sides of the bed hard. The doctor then proceeded to remove the baby by suction through the tube. I will never forget the horrific sounds of my baby being torn apart. I was screaming inside for them to stop! But it was far too late for that. In a matter of eight minutes, it was all over.

The doctor checked to make sure that he had gotten all of "it." He warned me that there would be heavy bleeding for several weeks, but that was normal. I could now get dressed and resume my life.

I walked out of that room feeling a total sense of loss. When I entered the lobby, it seemed that everyone was staring at me with knowing looks. At that moment, I felt dirty, like I would never come clean again. Bob greeted me with a smile in the waiting room and paid the $150 fee before we left. I felt dead inside. I had just done something that I never thought I would ever do. It went against everything I believed in, and now I could never go back. It was done.

Bob tried to convince me, "You did the right thing." *If this was the right thing, why does it feel so wrong?* This decision would haunt me the rest of my life, and he was over it in an hour. I was taken out to eat and shopping as promised, but I don't remember it. I went through the rest of the afternoon in a daze.

I waited a week and phoned my mother. "Mama, something's wrong. I started bleeding, and I'm scared."

"Get to the doctor right away."

"I have an appointment this morning. I'll call you later."

There was no way that I could bear to tell her the truth and break her heart. *I'll call her back in a few hours and tell her that I had a miscarriage.*

Our marriage was not what I had hoped for, and it was getting worse. I had been distant and depressed. One day, Bob and I had been fighting, so I went to visit my mom. Bob had written me a two-page letter and left it on the table when he went to work:

> *Our marriage seems to have gotten off on the wrong foot, which I feel is my fault. I'm sorry now that I wanted you to have the abortion. I realize now what a damaging decision that was.*

I handed the letter to my mother not remembering its full content. As my mom hit upon the word "abortion," she suddenly stopped reading and turned to look at me with a look that pierced right though me. "Abortion?" she said.

"I'm so sorry, Mama. I know how disappointed you must be. I didn't want to lie to you, but I didn't know what else to do."

She reached up and held my face in her hands. "Sister, I am really hurt that you lied to me, but mostly because you felt that this was your only option. I wish you would have come to me first. He made you do this, didn't he?"

I nodded my head yes. "He said that our marriage would be ruined if I didn't. I wanted him to change his mind, Mama."

Tears flowed from both of us, as she gently rocked me and tried to soothe away the pain.

The guilt of killing my own child was continually with me. Back at my house, I cried and pleaded with God, "Please forgive me! I have done an unspeakable thing! I'm so sorry that I have let you down. Please forgive me, Lord!"

I know that He forgave me the second that I asked. He promises to remove our sins as far as the east is from the west when we confess them, and to remember them no more! (Psalm 103:12) He forgave me of something when I didn't deserve to be forgiven; the problem was that I didn't forgive myself for many years to come. Every time we would drive by a billboard speaking out against abortion, the pain and regret would surface once again. They were painful reminders of my sin.

I heard on the radio that a man may become abusive or withdrawn from his children because he feels that he doesn't deserve to have them if he had been a party to an abortion. I hoped that this was not going to be the case with us.

I never would have gone through with the abortion knowing what I know now, even if I lost Bob because of it. Our marriage was not the wedded bliss that I had hoped for. He worked nights, and we rarely saw each other. My mother had told me "I feel that you married Bob to replace your father. He treats you more as a father would, than a husband should." But I didn't listen. *What do mothers know anyway?* In retrospect, she was absolutely correct. She was a very wise, discerning woman.

My grandparents worried what people would think, since we did not have a big church wedding. Their reputations were at stake. So Bob and I decided to have an "official" church wedding. We could have decided to have an annulment since we no longer "had" to get married, but we felt that we were in too deep.

We "wed" on November 15, 1980, with all the bells and whistles, including a new wedding dress, fancy cake, and tuxes. My grandfather escorted me down the aisle as my dad couldn't make it. It was a costly way to appease my grandparents. Bob surprised me with Amtrak tickets to Arizona to spend a week visiting my dad. I believed that he really wanted this marriage to work.

The train ride was enjoyable and relaxing, although I was still suffering the physical effects from the abortion. My dad greeted us at the train station, and he met Bob for the first time. They had a lot in common, and spent hours talking about law enforcement and guns. We had a great time visiting with my dad and his new wife. I enjoyed showing Bob all the things that I remembered from my childhood. I felt that it brought him a little closer into my life.

After the honeymoon, we moved to Geneva and Bob was hired by the police department. "I believe that a man should support his family, and the wife should take care of the home," Bob said. He worked on his parent's farm in the daytime and as an officer at night. I spent much of my time alone at the house.

Bob was an upstanding police officer. One snowy, Christmas Eve he was out on patrol. He had driven past a guard rail, and everything checked out fine. On his way back past the same guard rail, he noticed a hub cap on the road. He stopped to investigate and looked over the bridge into the creek. There, at the bottom of the creek, lay a car upside down. He called in the rescue team, but sadly it was too late. The two male victims had drowned in the icy waters. The families were appreciative that their sons were discovered and not left there, but it was still hard on him. "Why couldn't I have been there earlier to save them? They were so young, and I had to tell their parents the terrible news on Christmas Eve," Bob said.

"I'm so sorry," I said as I held him in my arms and rocked him.

Another wintry night, at about 2:00 A.M., Bob responded to a call of an accident on an overpass. A semi and a car had collided, and both had gone over the edge. The car had a female occupant, and he felt that she was still alive. The rescue squad assured him that she was deceased and left her lay on the cold pavement, while they tended to the truck driver. Bob was so upset that they hadn't even covered her up out of respect, so he found a blanket and gently laid it over her. Still, he refused to believe that she was dead.

"She's still warm. Let me take her to the hospital myself and have her looked at, to make sure," he pleaded.

"She's dead! Let us take care of her, and you take care of the accident scene," the EMT responded.

"A woman doesn't normally drive alone with icy road conditions at 2:00 A.M. I think that we should be looking for another person here," Bob said.

"No, it looks like she was alone in the vehicle," the EMT said.

"I can almost guarantee you that she wasn't alone," Bob replied, but it was so dark and the snow was so deep that he couldn't see. The winds howled and quickly covered up any tracks that might have been made.

By the time the female occupant was taken to the hospital, she was pronounced dead on arrival. Bob was extremely distressed about it and felt that more should have been done to take her to the hospital right away. The next day, at daylight, a man was spotted lying at the bottom of the hill. He had not survived the crash, either.

Bob had a way about him where he could calm down the most irate, belligerent person. He was a good man to call in to get a potentially dangerous situation under control.

When Bob and I were first married, we went on a vacation to the Black Hills in South Dakota. A buffalo reserve was nearby, and we stopped to admire all the beautiful animals. There was a huge buffalo standing near the road. Bob said, "Go over and crouch down in front of that buffalo. I want to get a picture of you two." I cautiously went up to the buffalo, which started snorting at me. I glanced back at Bob over my shoulder with a look of fear on my face. Bob assured me, "They are really gentle and totally harmless." Pointing toward the beast, he said, "Go on over there and kneel down." I ignored the snorting creature and crouched down for the photo.

Just as I did, a park ranger came running towards us, yelling at me, "Get away from that buffalo! They are very dangerous. You shouldn't be anywhere near him!" I got as much distance between the buffalo and myself as quickly as I could.

I glared at Bob. *What were you trying to do to me?*

He shrugged it off and said, "You were perfectly safe. He wasn't going to hurt you."

That's when I began questioning my husband's intentions for my well-being.

About two years after we were married, Bob surprised me with Amtrak tickets to Chicago. Neither of us had ever been there before, and we took a large blanket for the cold train ride. On the ride out, Bob asked me to have sex with him right there on the train seat, with other passengers in the seats ahead of us and beside us.

"I can't believe what you are asking me to do right out in public. Was that why you insisted that we bring a blanket along?" I whispered.

"People do it all the time," he said.

"Well, I'm not going to," I said, clutching the blanket closer to me.

"Then, I think we should just get a divorce," he replied.

"What? You want to divorce me because I won't sleep with you in front of a whole train load of other passengers, is that it? Why did you even want to go on this trip?" I asked.

"Things have been rough between us lately. I thought that it would be a way to start over," he replied.

"And so you pull this on me? All I want to do is jump on the next train heading back home. I don't believe this," I said.

"Look, I'm sorry. We're almost to Chicago; let's try to make the best of this trip," he relented.

A few months later, I suspected Bob was having an affair. He started coming home anywhere from two to three hours late every night saying, "Sorry I'm home so late, had lots of activity tonight." He was also mentioning a woman named Ann just a bit too often for my liking.

In the summer of 1983, I found out that I was pregnant again. Bob was once again upset with me. "We have only been married for three years. Shouldn't we have waited to start a family?" he angrily shouted at me before storming off. *But, I don't want to be alone all the time.*

It's ironic that I didn't marry my first boyfriend, Steve, for the very reason that he would never be home. My mother called saying Steve got on a local line as an engineer and was home every night. As it turns out, I married a man who was never home. Bob's dad was also a railroad man who was only home on weekends. I thought that I had chosen a life different than the one that I had grown up with. Why do we settle for second best, when God has the very best picked out for us? How different my life would be if I had just made other choices.

One day, Bob suggested, "We have been asked to go on a canoe trip this weekend with another couple. It sounds like a good time, and I think we should go."

I wasn't thrilled about going when I heard who the other couple was. Ann was the woman I suspected he was having an affair with. *I do not want to spend a whole weekend with that woman!*

Ann was deeply bronzed and perfectly toned, and I was a white, pregnant blimp. I closely watched how Bob looked at her, to see if there was any indication of an affair. He just looked at her the way that any man would admire a nice figure. She was in the lead canoe and rubbed herself with oil the entire trip. I spent the trip seething. Later that evening, the other couple suggested that we all get a hotel room together and share the cost. *No, absolutely not!* I was outnumbered 3-1 however, so I sullenly agreed.

An hour later, Ann suggested, "Lori, why don't you and I go swimming and let those men go into town?" Her husband and Bob were coworkers, and so they knew each other. I really didn't want Bob to leave me alone with her but didn't have much choice in the matter.

When we were alone in the pool, Ann confided to me, "You know, I have slept with every man in my hometown." She said it like it was a great accomplishment.

I vehemently replied, "My husband had better not be one of them!"

She flashed an innocent smile back and swam to the other side of the pool. *Why did she say that to me?* It did seem to confirm some of my suspicions about the two of them.

That night, she slipped into a slinky nightgown as I donned my tent. *She sure does make it a point to walk back and forth an awful lot in that barely-there nightie.* She and Bob even ended up in front of the mirror brushing their teeth together! They were sure cool about their relationship, if in fact there was one. *I can't wait for this weekend to be over.* Her husband was glued to the TV and seemed oblivious to anything that was going on. The next morning, we said our farewells and I returned home with doubts about my husband. *I wonder if he is one of the many men that she spoke of.*

❧

I was sick for most of the pregnancy and gained 68 pounds. Bob harped at me, "Did you have to get so fat? Other women don't seem to gain this much weight. Why did you?"

My head hung a little lower.

He continued on, "Obesity is something I will not tolerate. You look like a fat cow!" Instead of causing me to eat less, his comments had the opposite effect.

In January of 1984, I was overdue by several weeks. The doctor said, "I think we should induce labor. You have put on a bit of weight, and it isn't healthy for you or the baby. Let's see you back here at 7:30 tomorrow morning."

At 2:00 A.M. that night, Bob came home from work two hours late. I didn't take much time to worry about where he had been since I had been in mild labor for several hours. Bob timed my contractions for awhile and then fell asleep. My mother told me that I would be in labor for a long time, so I gathered my things and drove myself the two miles to the hospital. *I'll let him sleep until it gets closer to delivery.*

I arrived at the hospital and was escorted down the corridor to the labor room. The doctor checked how far I was dilated and told me, "If you want your husband to be here for the birth, he had better get here fast!"

Out of a dead sleep, Bob answered the phone. I quickly relayed the doctor's message.

Bob burst into the delivery room, still putting on his gown, just as our son was entering the world at 9:30 A.M. The nurse gently placed our beautiful son in Bob's arms, and he beamed with pride, gazing at him in wonder for a long time. "He's perfect, isn't he?" Bob said.

I was so relieved to see this change in him. *Everything is going to be fine. This baby is going to bring us back together.*

Throughout my pregnancy, I was always afraid to bring up the subject of the baby. Discussing what to name the baby was never brought up.

Baby Lang had no name for three days until we came up with Braden.

When we arrived home, Bob proudly took me around to see purchases he had made. "Look what I bought: a dehumidifier, a clean air purifier, and Clorox wipes. I want to have a healthy environment for my son."

It was rather comical to see how excited he was, but I was very happy that he was so pleased with our new son.

Three months after Braden was born, someone asked me, "When is your baby due?" I was mortified and knew I was going to have to lose that weight, which I did eventually.

I was a few inches shorter than Bob and 115 pounds when he and I met. I felt quite comfortable with my body. And Bob seemed to approve also, but he had always warned me, "I will not tolerate a fat wife." After we were married, he felt that I was unacceptably overweight. Every day, several times a day, he would remind me how fat I was. He jiggled my thighs to prove his point. I dieted to please him and I got down to 103 pounds, but still he complained. My mother was horrified when she saw how gaunt I had become. I finally decided that that was enough. *He is never going to be happy with me. I just have to be happy with myself.*

I continued to question Bob's fidelity; he was upset with me about my weight, the way I did the housework, and nearly everything else about me. In spite of the problems, we decided to have another child so Braden would have a playmate.

Bob drove me to the hospital and remained by my side the entire time. On May 5, 1986, after twelve grueling hours, Jamen came into the world. I was disappointed to see that the baby was a boy, but God handpicks the children that he gives to you. He saw my future beforehand and that I would need the boys' help more than I could possibly know.

On the way home from the hospital, Bob said, "Oh look there's Ann; let's stop and show off our new son."

No! I detest that woman.

He pulled up next to her at the gas station. Ann warmly congratulated me, to which I feigned a smile in return.

Braden was not thrilled with his new brother. They were totally different in personality, looks, and temperament. Jamen was easy going, with a big heart, outgoing and personable. Braden was the intelligent, methodical one, very mechanically inclined, and quite driven.

I always wanted that special mother-daughter relationship that I had with my mother. A mother's relationship with her sons seemed to be less intimate. I wanted to be able to fix my daughter's hair, and cuddle and talk with her. I looked at my children and wondered what their sibling would have been like had I not aborted. *Would it have been the little girl that I had longed for, with long, curly brown hair?*

A year after Jamen was born, an acquaintance of ours had two daughters. The older sister was a little girl with long, dark auburn hair and big brown eyes. Her younger sister was blonde with blue eyes. The mother was young and not very interested in being a mother. The girls were left with their grandmother, sometimes for months at a time. The grandmother decided to put them up for adoption, with the consent of their mother.

Bob and I decided to keep the girls on a trial basis. I needed to know if I could handle four children. I already had two children the same ages of these girls. Jamen had to be moved into Braden's room. Braden was already unhappy about having to share his things, and now he had to share his bedroom.

I was not working at the time. Bob believed that a mother should stay at home with her children, for which I was grateful but I didn't realize how much work four little ones could be. The younger sister had a constant runny nose, and she whined all day. The older sister had taken over the role of mother; she was very protective of her younger sister. She was a very quiet, obedient child, almost too obedient.

Bob and I visited with a lawyer about the legalities of adopting the girls. He said, "It would be roughly $150 for the paperwork, and the mother would have to sign the papers releasing them."

"That shouldn't be too much of a problem, if we can locate her. We need to discuss it a bit more and we'll get back to you," Bob said. I found out the following month how hard it was to raise four little children. They all wanted and needed attention, and so did my house. I felt like I was doing nothing but constantly cooking, cleaning up, and doing laundry, only to start it all over again.

After our one month trial, I spoke with the grandmother about adopting the girls. "I just can't handle this many children under the age of four. I would love to have the older girl. Would you consider splitting the children?" I immediately regretted asking this. Those girls needed each other; they were all that each other had.

"No, we won't allow the girls to be separated. They need to stay together," the grandma replied.

"I totally understand that," I said. "I don't think I can manage it, though."

"There is a doctor and his wife who have been inquiring about the girls lately. You have first choice since the girls have been living with you. So let me know if you want to allow them to adopt the girls instead," their grandmother said.

The doctor could offer them so much more than we ever could. They would be their only children, and have all of their love and attention.

The decision was very clear. We said our goodbyes to the girls and gave them back to their grandmother. The doctor and his wife adopted them, and I later heard that the girls were very happy. We had made the right choice. God knew what my future was to be.

One day, Bob and I were arguing. He went into the bedroom, grabbed his .357 magnum, and stormed outside. He waved the gun, wildly screaming, "I am just going to go and shoot myself!"

I paused for a moment. *He's got a loaded gun in his hand. Do I really want to chase after him?* I finally ran outside begging, "Please don't do this! Why do you want to kill yourself?"

"Life just isn't the way that I expected it to be. My own wife thinks that I'm having an affair," he cried.

"Well, are you having an affair?" I asked.

"Hell no, I'm not. You should know better than that," he said.

"Put the gun down and let's talk about it," I said.

He took the pistol back into the house, and the problem was solved for the moment. *Would he really have done it, or is this just some twisted little game that he's playing?*

Bob always told me, "If I ever find out that I'm dying of a terminal disease, I will be sure to take all of my enemies with me." One time when he was a policeman, he had a grievance with the mayor. He created a toxic concoction and secretly lined the mayor's coffee cup with it. He excitedly came home and told me what he had done.

My head reeled. *Should I call someone and tell them what he had done?* With the fear of repercussion, I remained silent. I was so relieved to later hear that the mayor didn't die. He was sickened from the poison but quickly recovered. Eventually, the mayor and Bob became friends. The mayor died years later of natural causes, and Bob was truly saddened to hear of his passing.

In 1987, Bob allowed me to get a part-time job at a local restaurant to help us attain the goal of owning a home someday. One evening, I called home and told Bob, "I'm going to be a little late at work tonight."

"That's fine," he replied.

Sneaking home, I crept up to the front window and peeked through the slit in the blinds. Just as I suspected, Bob and Ann were in an embrace on the living room couch. After composing myself, I burst through the door.

Under the weight of my glare, Ann quickly exited the scene.

Putting his hand up, Bob said, "Hold on. It's not what you think. Ann lost someone dear to her and I was just consoling her."

I hotly replied, "I know what I saw and consoling her was not part of it. Just admit it, you've been caught!"

An hour later, he confessed, "Alright! You're right. We have been having an affair."

Furious, I asked him, "So, how long has this been going on?"

"Five years," he solemnly replied.

"Five years! You've been sneaking around behind my back for five years! I was pregnant with both of the boys during that time! Ann admitted to me that she had slept with everyone in town. You could have brought home any number of diseases to me and the boys," I ranted.

"She's actually a very clean person, and there was never any danger to you or the boys," he said.

I was humiliated, and wanted to be as far away from him as possible.

"So, now what?" I asked.

"I love her, but I also don't want to lose my family," he admitted.

"So, you want us both. Is that it? I'm sorry, but three people in a relationship doesn't work for me." Pointing toward the door, I said, "I think you should leave."

Bob drove to his parents' farm and spent the night there. I went to bed and sobbed.

Now what do I do?

He came back home a few days later. *Maybe we can share the house and the kids, but live separately like roommates. I don't really know what else to do at the moment.*

After the affair was exposed, Ann was being very open about their relationship. She called the house nearly every day for months, just to chat.

When I answered the phone, she brazenly asked, "Can I speak to Bob?"

I held out the phone and yelled, "Bob, it's your girlfriend!"

He glared at me and grabbed the phone from my hand.

He talked to her like I wasn't even there. His world was neatly wrapped up. He had both of us, and to his relief, his dirty little secret was exposed so that he could quit hiding.

I didn't care anymore. I only felt disdain for him, but I stayed to keep the family together.

It finally dawned on me that Ann was the reason that Bob was so displeased with my weight. *Of course, Ann is a perfect size one.*

Bob had everything that he wanted so there wasn't any reason to change, but I had had enough!

I packed up the boys and filed for divorce. We moved to Hebron, Nebraska, where I rented a little house. Bob didn't take this arrangement well.

I received a letter in the mail one day from the Fillmore County Courthouse. I couldn't believe what I was reading: "You are hereby ordered to attend marriage counseling." *He has the nerve to order me to go to counseling!*

I had no choice but to attend the sessions. While I sat there, he told the counselor, "I love Ann so much. I could never give her up." He felt it only fair to be totally open and honest with me, about every sordid detail of their relationship. Every newly uncovered indiscretion created a larger wedge between us and validated my claim even more that this marriage was over. I was sickened by what I was hearing. *I can't believe that I had been such a fool!*

The counselor suggested, "Maybe you should quit seeing Ann and work on your marriage, if that is what you want to save. You might try going on a trip together to rekindle something."

"Yes, maybe that's a good idea," Bob said, nodding his head in agreement.

I don't believe this! A trip together? Are you kidding me?

I didn't want to be there, and he didn't want to give up his girlfriend to work on our problems. Counseling was totally pointless. Why did he want our marriage to work, if he wasn't willing to give her up? He wanted it all, but that wasn't a game I was willing to play. I silently endured all the court-ordered sessions, finishing with nothing resolved. He was so frustrated that I wouldn't see it his way.

I went home and resumed my life. Bob went back to Ann.

When Jamen was two, he needed surgery to repair a hernia. I made the appointment in Hastings, Nebraska, which was two hours away. We had to be there very early in the morning for the operation, so we drove down the day before and spent the night. Bob was there the next morning to stay with Jamen after the operation. It was extremely uncomfortable. We were going through our divorce, and we had to be stuck in the same room with our son the entire day. I refused to be the one to leave. I wanted to be there for Jamen. Bob tried so hard to smooth things over between us, but Ann was still in the picture and I was still hurt.

The divorce proceeded along. My mom, Gary, and I went to a child custody hearing, and as we were exiting the courthouse, Bob yelled, "The trunk of my car is full of guns! It's not fair that you should be allowed to have both of the boys! If you continue with this and don't allow me to have Braden, then you will be dead before you can make it down the courthouse steps! Do you hear me?" He spoke with such anger and determination that I couldn't help but believe him.

I avoided his gaze and huddled in close to my mom, Gary, and an officer. They escorted me down the steps, and I felt safe for the moment. Bob wasn't arrested for his threats, probably because he himself was an officer in that county. A strong brotherhood is formed among fellow officers.

I received threatening phone calls for the next few weeks from Bob. They all had to do with what he was going to do to me if I didn't give Braden to him. Fear became a constant companion.

My mother and I talked at length as to what I should do. She advised, "You are never going to be safe. He will not let this drop and go away. You will constantly be looking over your shoulder. The only choice I can see is to give Braden to him." I didn't like any of my choices. At that time, I had a two year old and a four year old. I had no money, and no job or skills. I thought of running away with them, but I knew that he would hunt me down to the ends of the earth.

After much debate, I decided to give Braden to him. At least, I could hopefully have some impact on Braden's life and be able to spend time with him this way; I would not be any good to him if I were dead. I gathered his things and, with great sadness, handed him over to his dad a month later. I can still see the look in his eyes when he said goodbye to me. How can a four year old comprehend what is going on and understand why you are telling him goodbye? *I'm so sorry, Braden. Mommy loves you! I wish it didn't have to be this way.*

I thought that I would be able to see him soon, on visitation. But every time it was my day to have him, Bob would take him away. I always looked forward to our visits and was furious when they didn't happen. The trip to the farm was spent with great anticipation of seeing Braden, and the return trip was spent sobbing. I did get to see him about every four months, but I was too afraid of Bob to go to the authorities. It got to the point where I didn't even know what kind of ice cream Braden liked, and I hated that. He was more like a stranger to me as time passed by.

One time when I finally got to see Braden, I asked him, "What have you been doing since the last time I saw you?"

Braden replied, "Daddy took me somewhere and we picked up a tombstone. It has all of our names on it, Mom."

Fear instantly overcame me. "You saw Jamen's name and your name on the stone?" I asked, not really wanting to hear the answer.

"Yep, they were all on it," he said confidently. *I can't believe that he would take our son and do something like that. Maybe he wanted Braden to tell me about it, to scare me.*

My life was consumed by the fear that Bob was going to kill all of us. I didn't sleep well at night; I was always listening for any sound. Why else would he have gone to the trouble to purchase a tombstone?

When we went to court once more for the final divorce hearing, Bob was clearly upset. After the judge declared how things were to be split, I quickly made an exit. Bob yelled after me, "This is not over! Do you hear me? This is not over!" Dina was watching Jamen at the time. I ran into the house and grabbed him, and took off in the car, making my way to Kansas where my best friend lived.

When Sheila answered the door, she was happy to see me but then quickly turned cold. I explained to her, "I am in trouble. Bob is after me. Can you put us up for the night?"

She angrily turned me away, saying, "I can't believe that you would put my family in danger like this. Please leave!"

I was so hurt that she would reject us. I would never have turned her away. She has not spoken to me since that day.

I drove on and on through the night, afraid to stop. I was constantly looking in the rear view mirror, never staying long on the same road. I didn't know if I was being followed. We ended up in Arkansas, when I decided that I could finally rest. I wanted to be gone for a while to let Bob calm down. Jamen and I stayed in out of the way places for the next ten days, until I felt it was safe to go back home.

Bob was ordered to pay me child support, of which I never saw a dime, so I had to work six days a week to support us. When I did happen to get Braden, a lot of times I had to work. I worked at a factory, and the pay was just enough to keep us going. Bob told me that if I forced the child support issue, he would quit his job or possibly move away with Braden, so I didn't pursue it.

Braden was five when he told me, "Daddy has been knocking me around. He picked me up and threw me into the wall." The thought of running away with the boys came into my mind more than once, but I was gripped with the fear of not being able to provide for them, along with the fear of never feeling safe.

I could be arrested since I was not Braden's guardian, and I feared the courts would use the fact that I gave Braden to his dad against me. I felt so trapped, so incapable of protecting my child.

I was thankful that Bob never asked to have a visitation with Jamen. At least, he would be safe.

Meanwhile, Bob was doing a lot of damage to his parents' home by punching holes in the walls and breaking objects. He got into an argument with his dad one day, and grabbing a pistol, he stormed out to the barn and shot his dad's bull. His dad wanted to throw him out of the house but didn't want to lose Braden.

I never felt so helpless in my life.

One day, I came home from work and discovered that my house had been broken into. Bob had gone through my closet and ripped up all of my nightgowns. I went directly to the sheriff's department and obtained a protection order even though Bob had previously told me, "I can shoot someone just as easily standing there holding a protection order, as not." Bob was ordered not to come within 300 feet of me. He watched my house from down the street instead. I never felt safe, constantly scanning my surroundings for any sight of him. Every day, I would come home to flowers on my doorstep. *You made your choice, now just leave me alone!*

Another time, Bob cut through the window screen of my house and hid in my closet. Jumping out at me when I came into the room, he wrapped a rope around my neck and tried to strangle me with it, leaving bruises on my neck. I somehow got away and ran to my mother's house, crying. She rushed me to the sheriff's department to file a report and have the marks photographed. Not wanting to be alone, I spent the remainder of the day at her house.

Looking much like The Rifleman, Gary stood outside their house holding a .22 caliber rifle. Bob showed up as expected and told Gary, "I just want to talk to Lori. I'm not here to cause any trouble."

While fixing the rifle on Bob, Gary firmly replied, "You already caused trouble. Now leave! I won't hesitate to shoot you."

Bob raised his hands in surrender, turned, and walked away.

Wow! This boy I previously loathed now stood as my unyielding knight in shining armor, my protector and defender. I was glad that we had resolved our differences long ago. He was someone that I was able to count on through many trials.

When Philip was telling me about the incident, I did have a faint glimmer of recollection of the sheriff's department. I believe that during trauma, a protective mechanism takes over, causing a person to block out memories. He tells me the story, but I have basically no remembrance of it, along with other stories that I have been told.

My ten-year class reunion was held in 1988 in Belvidere, Nebraska, with a meal and a dance. I drove up by myself and met my girlfriend, Jo, and her husband. We spent the evening laughing and reminiscing. Another classmate came up to me later, whispering in my ear, "Bob is just down the street, sitting there in his car, and watching the building. I just thought you should know."

Panic struck me. *I have to leave. I have to get out of here!* Jo and her husband quickly walked me to my car, and we said our goodbyes. I tried not to look around too obviously, to give him a clue that I knew he was there. I got in my car and raced home as fast as I could. I kept looking in my rear view mirror but never saw that he was following me. *He must have gone back home.* Bob and I talked about that night some years later. He told me that if he had seen me walking out with a man that we would have both been shot. *Oh my gosh, I could have gotten Jo and her husband killed that night.*

A year after our divorce, Bob sent me a letter:

Lori, I want you to know how wrong I have been. Ann isn't in the picture anymore. She seems to prefer married men. She even broke a beer bottle over my head when she left. I'm so sorry for everything, and I really want us to be a family again. I hope you will give me another chance. Please say that you will consider it.

Love, Bob

I wasn't interested in his apology. *How could I ever trust him again after all that he had done? The only reason he wants me back is because Ann is gone. Thanks, but no thanks.*

He admitted himself into the state psychiatric hospital, where he remained for a month. I later learned that he was diagnosed with manic-depression (bipolar disorder). The medications he was given didn't mix well. He walked around like a zombie for three months. He was unable to sleep, but walked continuously and shook uncontrollably. When he sat down, his body was in constant motion. During this time, he lost his job with the police department and was farming his parents' ground for a living. He finally weaned off of the drugs, a long slow process and vowed, "I will never take medication again, no matter how bad it gets."

THREE

A New Beginning

*For God has not given us a spirit of fear, but of power and of
love and of a sound mind.*
—II Timothy 1:7

In 1989, several years had gone by since the divorce. Bob went on with his
life and left me alone. He was living in a microscopic upstairs apartment
in Pierce, Nebraska, which was near the college he had been attending.
Braden was living with his grandparents on their farm. Each weekend,
Bob came home and helped with the farming.

Bob had always enjoyed cigars. One Father's Day, I was at the mall and
passing by a cigar shop. I thought of him—and I felt compelled to buy
him a few cigars. I carefully chose several kinds that I thought he would
like and took them with me when I went to get Braden on a visitation.
It seemed like fate. When Bob was on vacation earlier that summer, he
stopped at a trading post and had the jeweler make a heart-shaped topaz
stone into a necklace for my 30th birthday. I guess you never do quite get
over someone, no matter how they treat you.

On my next visitation day, I stopped at the farm to pick Braden up for
the weekend and Bob said to me, "I have been going to church, and my
life has changed. I would like to start over with you and our family."

He could see that I was very wary.

"I will prove to you that you can trust me again," he said earnestly.

We began dating again, very slowly at first. He and Braden came to
my house and we all played outside, riding bikes or going out for a walk.
It was good for him to get to know Jamen. He was everything I had wanted
earlier in a husband: thoughtful, attentive, and fun.

After several months, he invited me to his apartment. I picked Braden
up from Grandma's house and drove the three-hour trip to Pierce with

great anticipation. Bob's eyes lit up when we arrived. "I've been cleaning all week to make the place presentable. I'm so glad that you came," he said. It was nice to have the whole family together again.

On one of our dates, Bob came over to my house and brought a Bible along. He said that he would really like to start reading it with me. It was such a nice change in him. He never was one to go to church, and even though I was raised in the church, I had drifted away from God. I still prayed every now and then, but I did not have a personal relationship with God.

Through our time together, Bob proved to me that he could be trusted again, and I wanted so badly for the boys to be together. Bob had transformed into a man that I desired to be with.

We remarried on December 12, 1990. Things were great between us for the first year or so. He changed occupations, becoming a lineman for the power company. He was doing what he had always wanted to do, and was home every night. We were a real family, and I was happy.

We found a cozy place to live across the street from the grade school in Battle Creek, Nebraska. Unfortunately, snakes came out when there was a lot of rain. One day, when I came home, three snakes slithered across my kitchen floor and darted under the stove. A shiver went up my spine. Grabbing a flashlight, I cautiously peered under the stove. There were six beady eyes peering back at me, and I slowly backed away, and avoided the kitchen until Bob came home.

"There are three huge snakes under the stove. You have to do something," I squealed, jumping up on a kitchen chair.

He poked a broom handle under the stove and fished them out one by one, laughing at me the entire time. "They're just garter snakes. They won't hurt you."

"I don't care what they are. I don't want them in the house," I said.

We had cable TV and spent many enjoyable evenings watching Nick at Night and the Family channel. Everything seemed to be going our way.

Bob decided to surprise Braden with a go-cart one day. Braden couldn't wait to take it out and drive it around the homemade track in the backyard. Bob encouraged him with every lap. "Keep her steady, Braden.

Don't turn so sharp. Let up on the gas now." I enjoyed watching him spending time with the boys.

For Christmas, Braden really wanted a working steam engine that cost $350 and had specifically asked Santa for it. I was shocked when Bob (I mean Santa) bought it for him. Gift—giving was never a big thing with him. Braden treasured it. "Look Mom, you light this pellet right back here, and that's what makes it go." I watched as it burned a trail on the carpet, and everyone scrambled to stomp the fire out.

"Maybe we should run it on something less flammable next time," I said.

Life was good. There was just an inkling of the past: Bob didn't continue going to church after we were remarried, but I wanted the boys to go so I took them. After coming home, Bob accused, "Are you having an affair with the pastor?"

What? "You're crazy. How is it that I can be having an affair, during church, with our two sons, the whole congregation, and the pastor's wife there?" I asked him.

Not satisfied with my retort, he relentlessly pursued the subject. Every week, I endured the same badgering. He made my life so miserable. *I love the church, but this just isn't worth it.*

"Fine, I'll quit going to church, but not because I was doing anything wrong. I am just sick of your accusations," I told him. And Bob was happy.

My mother had a collection of children's Bible books that I read to the boys. They enjoyed hearing about the heroes in the Bible. After a while, this too went by the wayside. I regret that now and wish I had taken more time to teach my children about God.

FOUR

Abuse

Fathers, do not provoke your children to anger.
—Ephesians 6:4

Bob changed after our first year and a half of remarriage. He went from being fun to becoming a tyrant authoritarian. I have no idea what caused this change in him.

On a family outing to a department store, I separated from the guys when I went to pick something up. When I came back, I overheard Bob telling the boys, "Your mommy's dead and she's not coming back." I could see the looks from sympathetic women within earshot.

"My Mommy isn't dead!" Jamen screamed. "See, there she is."

"Why do you say things like that to the boys?" I asked.

"Because it's funny," Bob laughed.

"It's not funny. It's cruel," I said.

"Oh, they knew you were coming back. You have to admit it was funny. Did you see those women's faces?" he replied.

In October of 1992, two social service workers came to our house. There was a cowardly looking man in a suit and a heavy-set woman in a skirt. Her jowls reminded me of a bulldog, and the way she looked at me was just as intimidating. That morning, Braden had gone to school and complained of being hit by a belt. Both boys had been called out of class and inspected for bruises, but they found none.

Bob had always warned the boys that if they ever told about their punishments, they could be taken away from us.

The workers questioned both of us for hours. The woman asked me, "Have you ever spanked your child?"

"Yes," I told her honestly.

"What do you use to spank your child?" she asked.

"My hand," I responded, afraid of saying the wrong thing but equally afraid to lie. I couldn't bear the thought of losing my children.

Finally, Bob asked both of the workers, "Do either of you have any children?"

"No," each one said, looking Bob in the eye.

"Well, then how on earth do you think that you can tell me how to be a parent?" he demanded.

"Sir, you should never lay a hand on your child for any reason," said the woman.

"This is *my* home and these are *my* kids, and I'm not going to be told how to raise them by someone with no experience!" he bellowed.

I stood mutely by, afraid to interject, afraid to make things worse. At the same time, I was sure that, after his outburst, they would be taking the boys with them when they left. Thankfully, the moment passed, and the child protection workers finished their investigation. They left, leaving my family intact. I sighed with relief and felt the heavy burden of fear lift from my shoulders.

Bob was furious with the boys after the workers left. However, it had also given him a scare, and for a few months, he left the boys alone. He knew that they could be taken away, and he also worried about his reputation, knowing that it would be all over this small town in a heartbeat. I was so angry that my children had undergone a strip search because of him; the thoughts that were going through my head were making me sick. Jamen would have had no clue why they were dragging him out of class, making him strip, and looking at him. Thankfully, that was the only time that we ever saw the social service workers.

Oddly, teaching respect for me was of the utmost importance to Bob. "Do not ever talk to your mother that way again," he would say. Children somehow learn by example though, and when Bob spoke to me in a degrading manner, it was just a matter of time before the boys would follow his lead.

Times were intermittently good over the next few years. We bought a gorgeous acreage in the country. We moved a trailer onto the property to live in, and went to work on setting up the septic tank and utilities. We didn't want to be in debt so I got a job at the Farm Service Agency to help pay for the land.

Bob spent a lot of time in the pasture and found solace there. We purchased an egg incubator and obtained a permit to raise wild birds. Bob loved wildlife and wanted to repopulate the area. When he walked the pasture to check fences or spray weeds, the pheasant hens would become frightened and abandoned their nests. He also knew that the dog would go back later for their eggs. So he carefully gathered the eggs in his T-shirt and brought them home for me to incubate. For 21 days, it was my job to turn them twice a day. It was so exciting to see them start to hatch. When they were old enough, we released them.

At one time, we had a displaced California quail appear on our property. He took to our guinea hens right away, always falling in line after the pack. He roosted with them each night. Bob moved a large wooden crate into the hen house to make him more comfortable. He enjoyed watching him act like he was one of the guineas. One morning, Bob went out to the hen house to let them out for the day. The quail did not appear. Bob searched the room for him and found him dead, wedged between the wall and the new crate. He was devastated, "Why did I put that stupid crate in there? He would still be alive if I hadn't done that. Poor little guy."

Each year, Bob planted more than one hundred seedling trees on our property. We needed a windbreak, and he wanted trees that would provide fall colors. He planted each one carefully by hand and religiously took care of them. He wanted game birds to find refuge on our property, although he never hunted them or allowed anyone else to hunt. He planted different varieties of berry bushes so that they would have something to eat come winter.

Bob loved to watch sunsets and thunderstorms. He stood outside while lightning crashed all around, watching the clouds for a tornado in case we had to run since we had no shelter. During one particular storm, he loaded us all in the car at 11:00 P.M. and took us to Wal-Mart for safety until the storm blew over. It made me feel safe that he was watching out for us.

Summertime meant that the county fair would soon be here, and along with that came the lip sync contest. Jamen was a big ham and not afraid to be in front of a crowd. I worked with him and entered him in the contest, where he performed "Proud to Be an American" wearing Army fatigues and brandishing a faux rifle. He received a standing ovation from the cheering crowd. Each year, we practiced a new song. It took a lot of work to choreograph and learn to follow the song precisely. Still, Jamen worked on it until he was ready to enter the contest. He won several years in a row and was a natural entertainer. Instead of being happy, Bob fumed, "This is absolutely the last year. No more!" I never understood why. We always practiced when Bob was out of the house, so it couldn't have been that we were bothering him. Maybe it was that I was spending so much time with Jamen.

I learned to do things on my own and stopped asking for help. Bob built an addition onto our trailer, which we made into our bedroom. He failed to put a door on it, though. I didn't mind hiding behind the clothes rack to get dressed for the first year, but after three years of pleading with Bob, I bought a door. Bob was at work, so I got out the necessary tools and hung it up. I didn't put a doorknob on it, however, as I was afraid to attempt that project. I stood back with satisfaction and was quite proud of my accomplishment.

When Bob came home and saw the door hung up, he angrily shouted, "You should have waited for me to hang it. This isn't plumb! Now I'm going to have to redo the whole thing!" I opened and closed the door, demonstrating to him that it functioned. He stomped off in disgust. I asked him for the next year, "Could you please put a knob on door, so that I can dress in privacy, without the boys being able to see through the hole?" Again, I grew tired of waiting and did it myself.

Bob detested answering the phone. He sat right by the phone and let it ring, fearing that it was the electric company wanting him to come in to work. It was my job to screen the calls. Asking who it was, I would write

down the name and Bob would let me know if he wanted to talk or not. I am a terrible liar. "That didn't sound very convincing. Can't you do a better job of making up an excuse?" he scolded.

Bob loved his dog, Babe. He took her everywhere and was quite devoted to her. Whenever he would start up the four-wheeler, she ran and jumped up on the special seat that he had made for her. The boys and I hated her because she killed all of our kittens and kept us awake at night with her constant barking. *Why can't he show us the same kindness and love that he lavishes on that dog?*

He grew more controlling as the months went by. There were many things that weren't allowed. "I don't want you using deodorant or aluminum pots because they cause Alzheimer's. Jogging is not allowed because the jarring effect will cause wrinkles and your chest to sag. You will not go out in the sun without a full hat and sunscreen," he admonished.

Boxed food was not allowed; everything had to be made from scratch. Labels were carefully read for harmful ingredients. Ready-made pizza or spaghetti sauce contained sugar, so they were not permitted. No cooking was allowed in the summer; cold food would be prepared. Every winter, soup must be kept on hand at all times. Fat should not be removed from meat. He scolded the boys, "Don't cut that fat off! You eat all of that!" I felt bad for them. I tried to remove as much fat as I could before cooking, so the boys wouldn't have to endure the endless chewing of rubber.

I was reproached for dripping something, throwing something in the wrong waste can, or not cutting the tops off of the tea bags, because of the miniscule staple. Trash was sorted very specifically. Peelings were not to be thrown away but were for the mulch pile. The grass was not to be mowed so that it could re-seed itself. I didn't wash my hands correctly. "Are you able to wash your hands without splashing water? Look at this mess! Do you have to use that much soap?" he scolded.

Clothes were hung up to dry, never put in the dryer. "Only wash clothes in cold water. Don't fill the washer! Run just enough water to cover the clothes. Don't use all that soap! You don't need to put in the recommended amount. Let's try to do a little better, shall we?" I tried to get my chores done when he wasn't hovering over my shoulder reprimanding me.

To conserve water, toilets were only flushed when absolutely necessary. "We are not paying a water bill, so this seems a bit ridiculous," I said.

"Water is not just an endless supply. We need to do our part to conserve it, or one day, it will be gone," he said.

There were specific rules to follow about the thermostat. Winter temperatures were 50 degrees at night and no higher than 65 in the daytime. I was freezing all the time and bought an electric blanket to keep warm. Sometimes, I would look to see where Bob was and sneak over and turn the heat up to 68. Our bedroom had no heat, and in the winter, I could see my breath. It was not uncommon to have a thick sheet of ice covering the inside of the windows. The pipes were wrapped in heat tape so they didn't freeze. The air conditioner was only to be turned on when the outside temperature reached 90 degrees. "You should let your body grow accustomed to the heat and not pacify it with the air conditioner," he argued. I felt like a pioneer hacking it out on the prairie.

Road trips were agonizing. We were admonished to be looking out the window, enjoying the scenery at all times. Reading, sleeping, or playing games was not permitted. "You might miss something out the window that you will never see again," he would say. One year, we drove to western Nebraska for a job interview. We passed through two hundred miles of grassy plains, and everyone was so excited to finally see a snake on the road. "Sure glad we didn't miss seeing that," I grumbled to myself.

When Braden was in junior high school, all of the students were to learn a musical instrument, and Braden chose the trumpet. He beamed with pride as the salesman placed a trumpet case in his hands.

At home, Braden excitedly showed his dad the trumpet. "The teacher said that we have to practice for ten minutes each night," he said.

Bob scoffed, "Ten minutes, hah. That's not near enough time. I want you to practice for one hour every night. Do you understand?"

If Bob didn't hear the trumpet, he yelled, "Get back to work!" It didn't take long for Braden to hate the trumpet.

"I spoke to the teacher, and she said that ten minutes was long enough to practice without getting tired of it," I told Bob.

"Look! I paid for a trumpet, and it *is* going to be learned! Got it?" he thundered. He was right and I was wrong, and that was that. We returned the trumpet the following month. Bob felt that Braden had quit because he didn't take the time to learn to play it.

Every aspect of our lives was slowly controlled. He was upset with me when I didn't stand united with him on decisions because he was the head of the household and I should have respected that. Recently I read in my Bible, "When a wife yields her will to that of her husband, she yields to the Lord—provided the husband's directions are 'in the fear of God' or in line with God's will." In looking back, I know that Bob's actions were not in line with God's will. It also says to not be unequally yoked together with unbelievers. I was a Christian, and my mother warned me about marrying a nonbeliever, although with this last marriage, I thought he was a Christian.

Recently, one of the sermons at my church was on marrying a nonbeliever. The pastor told us that there is hope for women who marry nonbelievers by being the best wife possible. He explained that, "You cannot preach to an unsaved husband, because he cannot comprehend spiritual truths."

II Corinthians 4:4: "Demonstrate loving respect to your husband. However, this does not require agreeing to engage in sinful activities or living in fear. If your husband dangerously mistreats you, seek protection from authorities. Pray for you husband's salvation. In doing so, you are binding Satan and opening your husband's heart to the Holy Spirit." Admittedly, I was not the best wife possible. I did not pray for my husband as I should have, and I did not seek protection for my family when we were abused. I would hope that knowing what I know now, I would make better choices today.

One day, Bob decided that we were not allowed to watch TV, although he was. He bought a metal box to wrap the TV cord in and a combination lock. Whenever he wanted to watch the news, Bob would get into the lock box, plug in the TV, watch his program, and lock the cord back up. We were banned from the living room while the TV was on. *I'm treated like a child.*

Bob quickly discovered that the boys had figured out the combination, and he brought home different colored plastic locks and hid them in our bedroom. I would wait until he was away from the house and cut off the existing lock. We watched a TV show, and I replaced the old lock with a new one when we were done. I had to be sure to replace it with the correct color, though, so as not to be found out.

The boys and I enjoyed watching *Sabrina the Teenage Witch* each week. Jamen loved the talking cat. We waited for Bob to leave, cut the lock, and turned the TV on. I usually stood by the window on watch, while the boys quickly watched the show. One day, Bob had gone outside but not far. He noticed the blue glow of the TV through the window and came storming back in, yelling at me, "Just what in the hell do you think you're doing? Go behind my back, will you?" He whipped out his pocket knife, unplugged the TV, and with one quick slash cut the electrical cord in two, throwing down the severed cord. "I guess that's the end of the TV, isn't it?" he shouted as he stormed back out.

"You guys better stay in your rooms. I don't know how mad he is going to be when he comes back in," I warned the boys. When Bob came in that night, he knew that he had already won, so he left us alone.

The following day he chastised me, "Why do I always have to be the 'heavy' while you get to play the submissive parent?"

I silently walked away but pondered his words. *Maybe he is right. Maybe I am forcing him to be the bad guy. But why does he have to be such an unyielding dictator? He wasn't always this way.*

One day, Bob ordered, "Since there are three men in this house and only one female, when you are done using the toilet, you will put the toilet seat up."

The next time I refused to obey his order, he walked into the bathroom, ripped the toilet seat off the hinges and threw it in the yard. He smugly looked at me and said, "I guess we won't have a toilet seat then, and you will *not* replace it." We went without a toilet seat for the next year, until Braden got brave enough to put another one on that he had found. Surprisingly, Bob didn't say a word about it. He was probably equally happy to have a toilet seat again, instead of the cold, unyielding rim.

"I don't want you to hang out with divorced women," Bob said out of the blue.

"And why is that?" I asked.

"It's a chain effect, you see. When one woman gets divorced, her female friends are soon to follow. She starts to look differently at her own husband. For some reason, they like to commiserate together and compare notes, then the next thing you know, they are all getting divorced," Bob explained.

"Well, that doesn't really apply to me, since I am here with the boys all the time and don't have any female friends," I replied.

"Let's just keep it that way then," Bob said.

He purchased all sorts of exercise equipment, including bikes and elliptical trainers to help me with my weight problem, as 116 pounds was totally unacceptable. Grudgingly, I would use them for awhile to appease him, but they would eventually fall by the wayside. He was furious with me when they were turned into coat racks instead. "Why don't you do something about yourself? How could you let yourself go like this," he growled. My self-worth was destroyed by his continual berating. A kind word from him was never uttered, only criticism day after day.

It's ironic that, when we first started dating, he was pleased with me. *That one-pound weight gain must have really thrown him over the edge!*

I believe that his strong addiction to pornography had something to do with his actions. There was the constant comparison to perfection. I tried many times to destroy his stash of magazines, primarily to keep them out of the hands of my impressionable sons. Each time I hauled them out to the burn barrel however, Bob would see what I was doing and rescue them from the flames.

"What in the hell do you think you're doing? Those are collectors' issues!"

"Yes, and it doesn't matter where you hide them, the boys always find them. I really don't want my sons looking at this trash." It was no use. I might as well have tried to throw away the Hope Diamond. I was constantly being compared to perfect women, and deemed unworthy. He would see a girl with a nice figure and say to me, "Why can't you look like that?"

※

Braden was growing increasingly less tolerant of Bob's cruelty. He smiled while Bob yelled and hit him, which infuriated Bob more. It was a mind game that neither was going to let the other win. Jamen was a compliant child and never fought back, so Bob was not as hard on him as he was on Braden. He loved to grab a fist full of Jamen's hair when he was trying to get his attention, causing Jamen to wince in pain. I kept his hair cropped short so his dad didn't have anything to grab onto, but then he would grab his ear and yank on it instead. Bob got pure enjoyment out of tormenting Jamen. "Come over here Jim," he would yell.

"Stop it!" Jamen screamed. "Stop calling me Jim!"

Bob enjoyed figuring out what bothered a person and focusing on that. For me, it was biscuit cans and paper towel tubes. I hate the feel of the rough paper on my fingertips. He loved to grab my hand and rub my fingers back and forth against the paper, just to see me cringe. I never wanted to let him know what bothered me, or it would be used against me.

Walking on eggshells was a normal part of life. I kept my mouth shut, my head down, and did as I was told. I tried my hardest to keep the boys as quiet as possible, to not upset their father in any way. It was increasingly hard as Braden was becoming a man. He wasn't going to be pushed around, and it didn't help that he was three inches taller than his father.

"I don't think that Braden should be allowed to stay home alone after school. I can't trust him," Bob said. So each day, after school and during the summers, Braden would wander the streets of Battle Creek. He was too old for a sitter, unlike Jamen at that time.

"Braden is thirteen and has shown responsibility. Please, won't you let him stay home? I hate the fact that he has to run the streets all day. That's just asking for trouble," I pleaded.

"Well then, he can get a job to keep busy. I know of a guy who needs help roofing. I'll give him a call," Bob said.

The roofer set Braden to work, climbing steep roofs that were three stories high with no safety equipment.

"It's too dangerous to leave him at home unattended but fine to endanger his life on a steep roof? Not to mention breaking child labor laws?" I asked.

"He'll be fine. The work experience will be good for him and keep him out of trouble," Bob replied.

Despair was setting in. *What have I gotten myself into?* I felt bad for the boys having to live under such oppression.

Bob, having been a policeman, was sure that Braden was on drugs because he was becoming so defiant. Looking deeply into Braden's eyes, he said, "I can tell just by looking into someone's eyes if they are on drugs or not."

Braden stood steadfast and stared back.

I blurted out, "This is stupid! Braden is not on drugs. Leave the boy alone."

"Then why is he acting this way, if he's not doing drugs?" Bob asked.

Because you are so mean and this is his way of fighting back.

By this time, the boys were never allowed to leave the property. "I don't want them going to their friends' homes because there could be underage drinking going on," Bob said.

"Braden is a good boy. He's doesn't drink or smoke," I said. But Bob was growing more paranoid as time passed. He started searching Braden's room every day, looking for any concealed substances. Braden was becoming increasingly more defensive.

"Mom, I'm not doing anything wrong. I don't know why he won't believe me."

"I know you're not, Braden, but I don't know how to convince your father," I told him.

Finally, Bob removed Braden's door. He was not to have any privacy but was to be watched at all times.

Braden fought back by doing very poorly at school, even though he was extremely smart.

This added gasoline to an already smoldering fire. Good grades were acutely important to Bob.

"I want those boys to study *at* a desk for three hours each night."

"The boys have been sitting at a desk all day at school, and they need to burn off some energy," I argued.

Showing his authority, all unnecessary items were removed from Braden's room. It was to the point where he basically had a bed and a desk. Bob grabbed the back of the chair and harshly set it on the floor, advising Braden, "You will sit at your desk and do your homework. There won't be any of this laying around on your bed. Do you understand?" I didn't dare speak, but I felt that kids need to be kids, not under the constant watch of a supreme ruler. Their life was school and sleep, and to me, that was not a life.

I was afraid to step in when the boys were being disciplined. The few times I did made Bob much more enraged. The boys' consequence would then be a harsher punishment. My interference would set off something in him, which sent him totally out of control. Experience had taught me to wait until Bob had calmed down to talk to him. I learned to play the role of peacekeeper, much like his mother had. I tried to keep the kids away from their father and keep them quiet, doing anything to keep the peace.

Jamen was not terribly studious, and Bob wanted improvement in that area. He quizzed him continually at the dinner table and grew aggravated when Jamen didn't know the answers. "How do you spell 'special'?" he asked. I could see that Jamen was struggling with the answer, and I had previously taught him the alphabet in sign language. Standing behind Bob, I signed S-P-E-C-I-A-L, which Jamen repeated after each letter. He would avoid the wrath of his dad, and peace was maintained for the time being.

"Toys are a waste of time. These kids should be studying, not playing," Bob bellowed.

"I'm sorry, but I totally disagree. Kids need to play. Just look at Braden. He is so creative with Legos. He's built amazing battery-operated toys that can pick something up and bring it to him, long before the company came out with it. He's learning, not just playing," I argued.

"I want all of the Legos boxed up today, because I'm going give them away tomorrow," Bob ordered.

"You're going to give away hundreds of dollars worth of toys? Can't we just box them up and put them away?" I asked.

"Fine, but if I see one more Lego on the floor, they are out of here," Bob said.

The boys and I quickly gathered up the toys before he could change his mind.

Braden cut a hole in the wall of his closet and hid a small TV that he purchased from a garage sale in the wall. He told his dad, "I slid my bed up under the shelving for more privacy." Knowing why he had really done it, I was a party to his deception. The boys both had secret compartments for their hidden treasures.

Christmas and Thanksgiving were always a terribly stressful time. We had the same routine every year: go to Bob's parents' farm, and then the boys and I would go to my parents' home. Bob had no desire to see my parents, giving us some time away from him.

I looked forward to seeing my mother. One Christmas, Mama gave me a card with a cut-out picture of a sweater that she was knitting. "I'm still working on it, but I promise that you will get it someday," she said. I received it the following Christmas. I quickly slipped it on, and we burst out laughing. The arms hung clear down to my knees. "I love it! You worked so hard on it." I wrapped it around my waist to ward off the chill. "Thanks, Mama." We laughed a lot at my family celebrations. I don't ever remember laughter at Bob's parents' house. I just remember that I wanted to be anywhere but there.

I was so limited on presents that I could buy. "No toys," Bob warned. "They can have clothes, coats, and shoes or something that is absolutely necessary, but no toys. Everything has to be made in the USA, or don't bother even bringing it home."

"Do you realize how hard it is to find things that are made in the USA," I argued.

"Then we don't need it, do we?" Bob replied.

I got proficient at ripping off tags. I would sneak toys in and warn the boys to keep them out of sight.

One year, I purchased Jamen a Gameboy that he wanted for so long.

"You'll have to keep it out of sight, or your dad will take it away," I told him.

Later that night, the boys were playing with it in the bedroom at their grandparents' house. Bob entered and Jamen quickly slipped it behind his back. Bob saw the glow of the screen and ripped it out of Jamen's hands, waving it in triumph as he passed me.

Poor Jamen cried the entire way home from the farm. "Now do you see what you caused? You did this! This is all your fault!" Bob yelled. I felt terribly guilty. I kept looking back at Jamen and mouthed, "I'm so sorry." If I wouldn't have disobeyed orders, my son would not have had a ruined Christmas. I tried to be more careful with my purchases, although I still snuck in toys that were eventually discovered and taken away. When the forbidden items were discovered, and I was questioned, I lied and told him that Grandma had sent them a gift. I wanted my boys to have a childhood, to be able to just be kids, even if they only got to play with it for awhile.

I was certainly not innocent in all of this. I was not a loving wife, as most of the time I was acting out my frustrations. I did not feel needed, wanted, or loved. All I felt was controlled and owned. I lied to my husband, disobeyed him, defied him when I didn't agree with what he was doing,

and took the blame at times when the boys did something wrong. I knew Bob's wrath would be softer toward me.

Bob had been a good provider, however. At times, he could be very loving and fun. He was the "class clown" at work. "He is always such a jokester. Today at work, he picked up one of the other guys and was swinging him around on his shoulders. That was, until the boss walked in and caught him. He's so much fun," his coworkers would say.

I smiled and replied, "Yep, he's great," while wondering how he could be so different at home. *Why do they get the best of him? Why can't we see this side of him at home?* This was definitely not the man we knew. *He's never picked up the boys and playfully swung them around.*

I would look for ways to help Bob bond with the boys. I noticed in the newspaper that there was a small engine repair class at the college. *That would be perfect. Bob and Braden could work side by side with problem solving.* "What do you think about taking this class with Braden? I know he would love it."

"I really don't need something more to do," Bob replied.

"I know, but it would be a great way to spend some quality time with Braden, just the two of you. Won't you consider it?" I asked.

He sighed, "You're probably right. Go ahead and sign us up for the class."

I found a small engine in our junk pile, and they seemed to bond during their time together, still discussing their project when they arrived home. Bob got a little testy with Braden when he wanted to deviate from the way the instructor wanted things done, but all in all, it was a good experience for them. They never got the engine repaired, but that wasn't the point of wanting Bob to take the class.

At another time, there was a trap-shooting league that anyone could participate in. *Bob and Braden both love shooting guns. This would be another great way for them to bond.* But every week when it was time to go, Bob would say the same thing, "I'm really busy right now. You go on and take him." When we got home, Bob asked Braden, "So, how did the shoot go?"

Braden complained, "The stupid shotgun isn't shooting straight. I couldn't hit anything."

Bob scoffed, "It's a brand new gun! There is absolutely nothing wrong with the gun. It has to be the way you are shooting."

Braden tried to argue, "It's not my fault, Dad! That barrel is bent!"

Bob decided to go along with him the next time. He harped at Braden to do this or that, which made it hard for Braden to concentrate on the target. Braden was so miserable by the time that he got home, and Bob was satisfied that he had won the argument. "See, I told you that it was your fault and not a bent barrel," he chided.

Years later when we tried to sell the gun, we found out that the barrel was in fact bent.

In all fairness, I must say that Bob was very protective of his family. If anyone tried to hurt the boys or myself, he would do all he could to protect us. One night when we were first married, I was home alone sleeping when the phone rang. When I went to the kitchen to answer the phone, I saw a man peering in the window at me. I quickly dialed the police department and Bob showed up within minutes to gather what information I had. "The man looked like the same person that had been shingling our roof earlier this week," I said.

He took down the description of the man. A few hours later, Bob reported to me, "I found the guy. We had a very nice 'little chat,' and you won't be having any more trouble out of him." I breathed a sigh of relief.

Another time, Jamen came home crying, "Two boys were bullying me after school. They started hitting me and calling me names. I didn't do anything. I was just walking across the playground coming home."

Bob immediately called the police to file charges, "I want something done to these two boys. Those boys assaulted my son. I don't want to hear that they just got their hands slapped. I want them prosecuted. No one is going to hurt my kids." The county attorney took their young age into consideration, scolded the boys, and sent them home, and they never bothered Jamen again.

Bob preferred to stay home instead of being around other people. He would be quite content if he never saw another living soul, although at times, Bob did have a tender side to him. One night, we heard the devastating news that our neighbor had been killed in a car accident. Bob was the first one to go over and offer money and assistance to the widow and family. He repeated this act of kindness when another man was killed and left a family behind.

And when we were out in public, he was quite a different person. He was attentive and kept his arm around me, showing the world what a great husband he was. It was rather nice to have the "good" attention. Yet, I knew it was just an act and it would be over as soon as we got back home. Still, I longed for the "good" Bob to come around more often.

Each fall, Bob went deer hunting with his friend, Bill. They headed out to the western part of Nebraska and were gone for three blissful days. They had a wonderful time, and we looked forward to these trips with great anticipation. It was a time for us to be able to do what we wanted: to watch TV or have the toys out without fear of being caught. The boys could even go to their friends' homes. It was a time to let our guard down and have a good time. We enjoyed every minute of our freedom.

Bob called each night and I really enjoyed talking to him, as he was always sweet and loving on the phone. It was such a welcome change. *Why can't he talk to me this way when he is with me? Why does he have to be hundreds of miles away to be the husband I long for?* Maybe it was his way of keeping up a good face in front of Bill. But he seemed so sincere. We always dreaded the day of his return, though, as our vacation was over and it was now back to reality. I'm quite sure that he never got the big "Welcome Home!" from us.

Bob's motto about money was, "You can't take it with you when you die." We agreed to discuss any purchase over $30. Being in debt was simply out of the question, as we were trying to save money to build a house. By now, I was working at the Battle Creek State Bank and the Farm Service Agency. Most of the time, we were able to put my entire check into the savings account and live off of his paycheck. We were able to save money quite rapidly, taking advantage of the good interest rates the bank was paying at that time.

I was working the bank teller window one day when Bob drove up in the company truck and proceeded to yell at me through the window about something. Two women across the street heard his outburst and called his boss to complain. He came home later and told me with complete sincerity, "Do you want to know what happened to me today?"

I shook my head no.

"I was called into my boss's office, and told that I was yelling at you at the drive thru. Is this true?"

Thoroughly confused, I told him, "Yes, you did. Don't you remember?"

"I remember stopping to see you, but I don't remember yelling at you."

He paused to reconsider what had transpired earlier and calmly said, "Well, I had better go in tomorrow and apologize to my boss then," and he walked away.

This was a revelation to me. *Was he absent every time that he got upset? Where did 'Bob' go during these episodes? And where was my apology?*

There is a creek that runs through Bob's parents' pasture. One summer, his dad told Bob that he had built a cement dam in the creek. Bob argued, "You can't put a dam there. It isn't fair to deny the people downstream access to the water! What the hell is wrong with you?"

"You're not going to tell me what I can do on my own damn property!" Pointing toward the door, Grandpa yelled, "Get the hell out of my house."

Bob exited to the back room, grabbed some dynamite that he had been storing, and waved it at his dad as he stormed out the door. He drove out to the newly constructed dam, carefully placing the dynamite where it would do the most damage. Lighting the fuse, he ran for cover. The explosion could be heard back at the farm. His dad drove out to the site, and the two of them got into a screaming match. He was furious with Bob but never replaced the dam.

Bob seemed to be the man in charge of everyone else's life but his own.

He thought that counseling would help figure out why Braden was being so defiant about school. I found a competent, grandmotherly counselor for Braden named Mrs. Layton. Braden, Jamen, and I went to the first session. We explained what our lives had been like for the past several years. Mrs. Layton asked questions and took notes. When we left, she said, "Next time you come, please bring your husband along. I would like to talk to him also."

The next week, all four of us went to her office. Bob and the counselor greeted one another, and then he asked, "Do you have any clue what's wrong with Braden?" She in turn started firing questions at Bob, "Do you have trouble with sleeping, isolation, fatigue, or appetite?"

Bob grimaced, and then snapped back at her, "Are you suggesting that I am bipolar?"

"Yes, I am," she calmly replied. "You see," she continued, "Bipolar is an imbalance of key chemicals that change the chemistry of the brain. It can, however, be easily treated with medication."

"Yes, I know what bipolar means, lady!" he retorted.

Her words struck me. *Of course. It all makes sense now. He told me about battling with this year's ago.*

I never knew if Dr. Jekyll or Mr. Hyde was coming in the door. It was such a relief to see Dr. Jekyll come home, although it could change at any moment and generally did. I also knew that if we had a really good day, we would pay dearly for it the next. Two good days in a row were virtually nonexistent.

"Well, we are not here for me, now are we? We are here because of Braden," Bob stated.

"That's exactly what I'm trying to explain to you," she said, while leaning a little closer to Bob and looking him straight in the eye. "Braden isn't the one that I'm concerned about at the moment. If we can help you, it will in turn help Braden."

Before we left, she wrote Bob out a prescription for antidepressants. I was relieved that maybe, finally, we could have our lives back, but he angrily threw away the prescription and ushered us out of her office. He screamed the whole way home, "What on earth did you tell her last week? That I was some kind of a nut case?"

I couldn't shrink far enough away from him. I just wanted to get home and get some distance from him.

I honestly believed if he had been on medication, he would have been fine. He was a good man; I had seen that side of him. He was very well liked by everyone; he was just a different person at home. It was a matter of control. When he didn't feel like he was in control, that is when the problems started. He seemed to be able to turn it off and on at will; otherwise, why was he totally different at work than he was at home? He felt safe to be his true self with us.

"I refuse to be on medication again! I remember what it was like when the doctor had me all doped up. I was a walking zombie. It made my senses dull and sluggish. I am never going to go through that hell again. Besides, Braden is the problem here, not me!" he said harshly.

Great, now we all have to suffer! The therapist was deemed a quack, and we never returned.

FIVE

Mama

Who can find a virtuous woman? For her price is far above rubies. Her children rise up and call her blessed, her husband also, and he praiseth her.

—Proverbs 31:10

Mama and I took the boys to the swimming pool one summer's day in 1995. The temperatures were sweltering, and we couldn't wait to soak our feet in the cool water. But when Mama tried to step out of the pool, she found she couldn't lift her leg. "I've been noticing some problems with it being limp lately," she confessed. "I have an appointment with the doctor on Monday."

"I suspect that it might be multiple sclerosis but can't be sure without further testing. I'm sending you to Omaha for an MRI and spinal tap," the doctor said.

At Omaha, the tests came back inconclusive. "I think we are going to have to send you to the Mayo Clinic in Rochester, Minnesota," Dr. Meyer said. Three weeks later, I dropped the boys off with Bob's parents, and Mom and I headed to Rochester.

We checked into our motel and a shuttle took us to the clinic. The clinic was amazing, almost like a little city. Finding our way to the check-in desk, we were handed a schedule of her appointments for the next three days. She had anywhere from three to five appointments each day. We tried to make the best of our time there, finding many things to do in between appointments: going to the movies, shopping, dining, or going to the bookstore. It was a wonderful way to divert our attention for the time being. We traded in Mama's walker for a wheelchair to get around the expanse of the building.

Back at our motel, we sat on the bed playing cards and talked about all that had happened that first day. "I'm so tired of all the painful testing. I just want to go home," Mama said.

"I know you do, Mama, but we need to find out what's wrong with you," I assured her.

The second day of testing brought a conclusive diagnosis. The doctor gently told her, "You have a terminal illness called Lou Gehrig's Disease."

Mama tried to comprehend what he was saying. "I'm dying? That can't be."

I was brought in from the waiting room and told the news. I couldn't speak. *No! You're wrong. She has multiple sclerosis.* I finally snapped out of it and spoke up, "She stepped in a puddle of termite spray a few months back that contained chlordane. Could that have anything to do with her diagnosis?"

"It's impossible that she got Lou Gehrig's from the termite poison," he replied.

"Why couldn't it be possible? It kills termites by attacking their nervous system doesn't it?" I asked, searching his face.

"I'm sorry, but termite poisoning does not cause Lou Gehrig's," the doctor said.

"How long does she have?" I asked.

"Anywhere from three months to seven years," he replied.

At the age of sixty, she was so young and healthy. *This shouldn't be happening!*

We wearily went back to the motel and I called Bob with the devastating news, "Mama is dying of Lou Gehrig's."

"I'm sorry, Baby, is there anything they can do?" he sympathized.

"No nothing. We'll be heading back home tomorrow," I said.

"Okay. Tell your mom, I'm really sorry," he said.

Not knowing what we were dealing with, we went to the clinic library to educate ourselves about the disease. I knelt beside Mama's wheelchair and read, "Lou Gehrig's disease, also called amyotrophic lateral sclerosis (ALS), causes the nerve cells in certain regions of your brain and spinal cord to gradually die. Eventually, people with the disease lose the ability to move their limbs and the muscles needed to move, eat, speak, and breathe. Patients become paralyzed and often require ventilation and surgery to provide a new opening in the stomach (gastrostomy). Loss of respiratory function is ultimately the cause of death." I looked up at Mama and saw the despairing look on her face. The more we read, the more frightened we became. It seemed such a horrific way to die.

"Stop reading," Mama said. "I don't want to hear any more right now." Deep in thought, she finally broke the silence and said, "What will Gary would do without me? And the kids? What will they do?" It had always been her job to take care of everyone.

Why, God? Why are you letting her die? I just don't understand! Please take this disease away from her.

It was a long drive home. There was so much to talk about; so many plans to make. We tried to be positive, but the outcome was so grim.

Mama was approved for disability and received an electric scooter, and a rail that moved along the ceiling from room to room that could lift her into her chair or allow her to use the bathroom. A Home Health nurse was hired to stay with her during the day.

I was able to visit every month or two. Mama grew noticeably weaker and more paralyzed each time I saw her. The disease was slowly creeping up her body.

I did some research, and found that chlordane was banned due to damage to the environment and harm to human health. It affects the nervous system, the digestive system, and the liver. I was convinced that this had something to do with her contracting the disease, no matter what the doctor said.

Mama's dream was to see the Precious Moments Chapel in Carthage, Missouri, as well as visit Branson, Missouri. She had a vast collection of Precious Moments figurines. We decided not to wait and headed south the following week. She drove a lot of the way, with the assistance of hand controls to regulate the speed and brakes. Mama really enjoyed the

Precious Moments Chapel, and I was happy that I was able to share it with her.

Afterward, we stopped at the Thorn Crown Chapel, located in the mountains outside of Eureka Springs, Arkansas. The chapel is made completely out of glass. When sitting inside, you are surrounded by the majestic forest. It was so peaceful, and we began to pray, *God please take this illness from her. Please bring a cure in time to save her.* We felt, in this special place, that surely God would hear and answer all of our prayers.

With newfound optimism, we decided to explore the town. "Oh look!" Mama cried, pointing to a mountain of beautifully colored slag glass. "Let's stop and buy some."

I stood in that pile for what seemed an eternity, holding up one rock after another until she made her choices. Thinking back on that day brings back fond memories and I wish I could go back and do it again.

When we returned home, she made an appointment with the dentist to get her teeth cleaned. I asked, "Why do you want to put yourself through that?"

She replied, "I could live for another seven years, and I want to take care of myself. Besides, a cure could come along any day." She was so encouraged each time there was news on the prospect of a cure.

She never lost faith in God, praying constantly that He would heal her. Friends came over to pray with her. I stayed in the background and didn't participate in the prayers. It would have meant so much to her, but to me it was awkward and foreign. She wanted so badly to hold onto life, not wanting to leave her family. She was on oxygen, and the ability to breathe and eat grew increasingly more difficult.

One day, she asked me, "Of all my things, what would you like?"

"I would love to have your stuffed animal, Ferdinand the Bull, and *The Story of Ferdinand* book. They were special to you and would mean a lot to me," I said.

Ferdinand is a gentle bull who would rather smell flowers than fight the matadors. Maybe that is why I loved the story. I was tired of fighting matadors.

One day in 1998, two and a half years after her diagnosis, Gary called, "Your mom passed away in her sleep last night."

"No!" I screamed. "She was supposed to live awhile longer."

"You really didn't want her to go on living like that," Gary said.

"But I need her. We all do," I pleaded.

"I know, but she needed to go home," he gently replied.

I hung up the phone and ran outside, sobbing uncontrollably. I wanted to escape this reality. *Why did you take her, God? Why? You could have healed her!* Bob held me, softly caressing my hair with his hand. "She's gone. Mama's gone," I cried. He allowed me to cry and pressed my head gently to his chest, trying to soothe away my pain.

Mama didn't want anyone burdened with planning her funeral, so she made all of the arrangements. Her "going home celebration" was just the way she wanted it. She chose the song "The Anchor Holds," wanting everyone to know that through her illness, her faith remained strong. She had not wavered and knew that God had a purpose in this. She always said, "It will be all right. God is in control, and He can heal me if He chooses to."

I was devastated. Mama and I were more like sisters than mother and daughter. I had lost my best friend. It was so hard for me to go to the funeral home and see her. *This isn't how I want to remember her.* I stood back from the casket, trying to distance myself from the reality of who was inside. Gary took my hand and dragged me to her casket. I kept my eyes on the floor and tried to pull away from him. *No! I don't want to go. Don't make me go up there.*

He gently said, "Look at her, just look at her." When I forced myself to look at her, I realized that "she" wasn't there. This was a façade that I was seeing. My mother was with the Lord, laughing and walking for the first time in years. With new boldness, I leaned in and whispered to her, "Take care of my baby until I get there."

The family sat around laughing and talking, with my mother to the side. I think she would have enjoyed seeing us all together, enjoying each other's company and sharing all the wonderful times we had experienced with her.

The funeral was simple, and she was laid to rest in Kansas next to her parents. She loved cardinals so we lined her casket with beautiful red birds. She chose a black, heart-shaped head stone to commemorate her life. Bob never left my side. He held me and allowed me to mourn. I was glad to have him there.

I missed Mama terribly for the next year. Bob was very compassionate of my loss during that time. He knew how much she meant to me. I found myself going to the phone to call and tell her something. With my hand on the receiver, I would suddenly remember that she was gone. She probably already knew what I was going to tell her. I now believe that she was taken out of my life at that time, so that I would learn to depend on God for help instead.

Today, I have wonderful memories of this incredible woman. She was honest, and a woman of virtue. In her final days, she was scared and didn't want to leave. She wanted to stay for her family. I never got to see my mom grow old, as she was only sixty-two when she died. I look around at gray-haired grandmothers out with their daughters, and I feel cheated. God, however, had numbered her days from the time she was born. She had fulfilled what she was sent here to do, and it was time for her to go home.

SIX

And So It Continues . . .

There is no fear in love; but perfect love casts out fear, because fear involves torment. But he who fears has not been made perfect in love.

—1 John 4:18

Bob listened in on this psychiatrist's radio show every afternoon for its entire three hours, and every day, he would ask, "Did you listen to her program today?"

My answer never varied, "I don't get radio reception at work, which is where I am each day from 1:00 P.M to 4:00 P.M."

He angrily shot back, "I'm going to divorce you if you don't start listening to her program!"

Fine. Divorce me. I really don't care anymore.

He brazenly said, "She is the perfect woman. I would marry her if I could!"

I flatly replied, "She wouldn't want you." *I wish that you would run off and marry her. It would serve you both right.* She made my life a living hell. Anything she said that day was the way things were going to be done. For instance, she advised searching your child's room, so every day, we endured that, although Bob never found anything incriminating.

This went on for months. One day, I was in the house cooking when Bob came in to make sure that I was listening to her program before going outside with his own radio blaring. She had a caller that had a husband like Bob. Her response to this woman was just as I had hoped. "This man needs professional help for his behavior."

I ran outside asking him, "Did you hear that?" No, so I repeated the exchange.

"I hardly believe that she would say something like that," he replied, walking away.

I tried to call her show, to get on the air and have him actually listen to what I was saying and have her give the reply that I longed for him to hear—that he was driving his family away with his tyranny. But it never happened.

Every day, no matter whether it was during the week, on the weekends, during the summer, or holidays, Bob forced me and the boys to wake up at the crack of dawn. After breakfast, he would disappear into the seclusion of the pasture for the day. Meanwhile, I was left with two grumpy kids, with no TV to watch and no toys to play with.

Winters were hard when the weather was bad, and the boys were stuck inside the twelve—foot-wide trailer for months at a time. Summers were just as bad because Bob was constantly yelling at them, "Get off the driveway. I'm trying to let the grass grow, so get off!"

"We drive on the driveway, therefore the grass is not going to grow there," I argued. *It's just another excuse to scream at everyone.*

Any given day, the boys could be found sitting on the porch playing with their cats, which infuriated Bob. "Get those cats away from the house!" he yelled. Finally, he built a pen. "If you want to play with your cats, you will have to go inside there and play with them, but I better not ever see any of them out here again!"

"Why do they have to be caged, Mom? They weren't doing anything wrong," Jamen asked.

I had no explanation to offer.

We purchased a Welch pony for the boys and named him Dusty. He had been confined to his pen for several weeks, so I decided to take him out for a walk with the lead rope. Jamen and Babe trailed along. Dusty was fine on the way out, but on the way home, his pace picked up, and he began bobbing his head and snorting. He kept getting farther out on the lead, until I was just barely hanging onto the end of it. I was struggling to hold onto him, not wanting him to get away from me on the busy road. Suddenly, Babe leaped out of the ditch, and Dusty bucked, catching me in the cheek with one hoof and the ribs with the other. Everything went black, and gravel imbedded itself into my hands as I hit the ground.

Jamen ran frantically home to get help. I woke up and managed to get to my feet. A pickup was driving toward me, and from it, I could hear Bob yelling harshly, "Get in the pickup!"

I wasn't about to get in that pickup, waving him away.

"You get in this pickup now!" he screamed louder.

"No," I said, as I staggered the rest of the way home.

He drove alongside me, berating me, "What the hell is wrong with you? How could you let something like this happen?"

I was nearly killed. Is there not one ounce of compassion for me?

"I'm going to go out and shoot that damn horse!" he decided, pulling out his pistol.

"Don't shoot him! It was Babe that spooked Dusty, and it was my fault for taking him out when he was so wild. Please don't shoot him." I pleaded, and Bob reconsidered.

"I can't believe you were stupid enough to get hurt. Just look at you. Let me take you to the hospital," Bob growled.

I didn't want him taking me anywhere, as angry as he was. "I'll be fine. All I need is an ice pack," I said. I hurt everywhere. Standing in front of the mirror, I was a gruesome sight. *But thank you, God, for protecting me.* Had Dusty's hoof hit me an inch in any direction, I would have lost an eye, ear, nose, teeth, or even my life. His hoof hit me directly on the cheekbone. It was not just a coincidence.

Hugging me, Jamen said, "I was so scared, Mommy! I thought you were dead. I tried to wake you. Then you started mumbling and I ran to get Dad."

At least someone cares if I live or die. I slipped my arm around his shoulder, "Thank you, Jarmie."

When I woke up the following day, my face was hideously swollen and every shade of purple. Through tiny slits, I found my way to the car and drove to the clinic. I looked like someone had beaten me, which is exactly what the doctor thought. I assured him, "Our horse kicked me. See the gravel in my hands from trying to catch myself when I fell?"

Not quite convinced, he ordered x-rays of my face and ribs. My face amazingly was not fractured, although I had a mild concussion and one of my ribs was broken. I was sent home with a prescription for the pain to help me get through the next six weeks of healing.

When it was time for me to return to work, Bob worried, "Now everyone is going to think that I did this to you." *A man of upstanding character would not have to be concerned about his integrity being questioned.*

One day, Bob suggested, "I think we should have another child."

I scoffed, "You already have two children that you don't pay attention to. Why on earth would you want another one?"

"Next time, it will be different."

I found that nearly impossible to believe. Besides, I had already had a tubal ligation done a few years before. I didn't want to put any more children through what the boys had endured.

Bob knew that our marriage was in serious trouble again and figured that if we had another child, I would be bound to him and unable to leave.

By this point, I don't remember laughter in our home. We were too busy being scared, cautious, upset, or walking on eggshells to have any fun. It was a sad existence. If the truth be told, that's all it was, an "existence."

Our lives were a nightmare. Bob had to be in total control at all times. I had no value, was hopelessly defective, and unworthy to exist.

I prayed so many times, "Dear God, please take him from our lives, so that we can live in peace."

While at work one day, Bob's coworker approached me with a somber look on his face. "There's been an accident. Bob was electrocuted today by an arc while standing by a utility truck."

Good! I thought coldly.

He continued, "He was taken to the hospital in Neligh. The doctor said he will be fine."

Why didn't you let him die, God?

"I will take you to the hospital," he offered.

"I appreciate that, but it won't be necessary," I replied. He left, looking confused.

He probably thinks I'm a horrible person. Maybe I am. I finished out the work day. My coworkers shot questioning looks to each other but said nothing. At the end of the day, the boys and I went home. I told them about the accident but didn't receive a reaction in return.

Later, the phone rang. "Could you bring over a change of clothes?" Bob said.

No, I was really looking forward to a peaceful night at home.

"And could you bring me a chocolate shake?" he said, with hint of excitement.

"A chocolate shake and clothes, sure," I said without inflection. We arrived at the hospital a few hours later.

Bob was so happy to see us and told us all about the events that had taken place up to that point. He never asked why we hadn't come earlier. It probably didn't need to be said. "I should be released tomorrow."

Maybe this gave him enough of a scare and he will be a different person when he comes home. If there was any change in him, it was short-lived.

I prayed so many times for him to go to work one day and never return. *How hard would that be, God? Just take him out of our lives.*

SEVEN

God Help Us!

Be strong and courageous. Do not be terrified; do not be discouraged, for the Lord your God will be with you wherever you go.

—Joshua 1:9

He will give His angels charge over you.

—Matthew 4:6

It all came to a head on September 17, 1999, when we decided to flee.

After talking to a friend, Maureen, about our situation, she offered us a place to stay about ten miles away in Meadow Grove, Nebraska. Her sister had a rental house that would be perfect. We needed time and space to consider where we would go from there. When we got home that afternoon, we packed up the station wagon and van as quickly as we could. We had approximately two hours before Bob would return home from a jobsite. We snaked our way through deserted country roads in an attempt to avoid him. Under no circumstances did I want to meet up with Bob now!

Braden was fifteen, with a learner's permit, and driving the station wagon. Jamen and I were in the van. I looked at the clock on the dash: 3:30 P.M. *He could be anywhere right now.*

My heart raced when we saw a utility truck approaching. *NO! It can't be! Please don't let it be Bob!* With nowhere to run and nowhere to hide, fear and panic gripped me.

As the truck drew nearer, I could see Bob, an angry expression on his face. I knew that look all too well. He slammed on the brakes and swerved in front of us, cutting off our only path of escape. Bob jumped out of the truck and screamed, "What on earth are you doing? Trying to steal my kids, are you?"

Terrified, I kept my eyes downward and managed to whisper, "We just needed a little time away."

He waved his arms and screamed back, "Time away? Time away from what? You are so pathetic! I treat you like a fucking queen, and you turn around and do this to me! You bitch!"

I trembled from head to toe, immobile and vulnerable. The kids looked on, horror on their faces. *How on earth are we going to get out of this?*

He stormed over to the station wagon, ripped open the door, and jerked the keys from the ignition. Raising them in the air in triumph, he went over to the van, lifted the hood and yanked the distributor wire. He stuck his finger in my face and said to me through clenched teeth, "You had better stay put, bitch!" With gravel flying, he sped off to take the company truck back to work.

Braden had another set of car keys hidden away and begged, "Please, Mom, come with me! Please! We have to get out of here *now* before he comes back!"

I quickly considered my options. "I can't Braden! I'm just too scared of what he will do to us. I have already upset him enough."

I couldn't think rationally under all the duress and was so afraid of what he would do not "if", but "when," he found us.

"Well, I'm not going to be here when he returns!" With one final plea, Braden begged, "Get in the car and come with me, please Mom!"

I shook my head no. "You better get going before he comes back."

Braden jumped in the car and sped away as fast as he could. Jamen and I waited, not knowing what to expect next. "What do you think Daddy will do to us when he comes back?" he asked.

"I don't know, Jamen." Horrible scenarios were going through my mind. *I should run. I should get out of here. I should have left with Braden.* I quickly surveyed my surroundings, but there were no houses and not a single car had come by.

Then I saw Bob's pickup barreling down the road toward us. I've never been so scared in my life. *I should have gotten Jamen out of here. Why didn't I send him with Braden?*

Bob noticed that the car was gone and flew past us, trying to catch Braden. Giving up the chase, he drove quickly back to where we were. He grabbed Jamen and put him in the truck. He unloaded all the contents of the van into the back of the truck, all the while screaming, "This is mine! This is mine!" He threw the TV up against a post smashing it. All I could do was watch. *What's he going to do with us?* I thought my heart was going to pound out of my chest.

Seizing me by the arm, he dragged me around to the front of the van. He opened the hood, grabbed me by the hair, and pushed my head down into the engine, crushing my head in his hands.

"*STOP IT,* you're hurting me!" I screamed.

He pulled the hood down to slam my head with it but stopped when he saw Jamen looking at him from inside the pickup. Without Bob seeing, Jamen signed to me that he was going to try to make it to his friends' house by spelling out D-A-N. I nodded ever so slightly that I understood.

We both knew that I would not be making the trip with him.

At around 4:25 P.M., Bob took off with Jamen, leaving me there. I helplessly watched as they drove down the road, praying, "God, please protect my baby. Don't let Bob hurt him! Please God." I wondered what my fate was going to be. *He will have to come back for me sometime. What will he do to me then?* My mind raced with all the possibilities.

I heard gunshots in the distance. There was a black powder shoot going on that day, just a few miles from where I was. *I could run to them for help. Here was a whole group of men with guns, they would protect me.* But he had my son, and I didn't know if he had gotten away. Not knowing what else to do, I stayed with the van.

In the van, I noticed two items that Bob had left behind: my Bible and a .22 caliber handgun that he had purchased for me for protection. I checked to see that it was loaded. *Good, I have nine shots.* I slipped the gun into my pocket.

Hours dragged by. I prayed, "Lord, please let someone drive by and find me. Please send someone to help me!" I couldn't believe in all that time that not a single car came by. In looking back, I could see that it was not in God's plan for me to be discovered.

Eventually, I fell asleep in the back seat. I awoke to the sound of a vehicle skidding to a stop.

Bob jumped out of the truck brandishing a Ruger Mini 30, screaming, "Do you see this? I have one thousand rounds of ammunition on the dash, to deal with you, you fucking bitch!" Waving the rifle around, he yelled, "I could kill you right here and now. Do you hear me?" Grabbing me by the arm, he shoved me into the truck and drove home, leaving the van there. The whole way home, he drove like a maniac, and said, "Maybe we will both die in a car accident. Wouldn't that be nice to leave the kids as orphans?" He swerved wildly back and forth over the road.

I had no idea what time it was when we arrived home. It was still light enough, however, to see that he had shot all the cats. "Why on earth did you kill the cats?" I said, trying to keep from screaming at him.

He simply stated, "Because you abandoned them, that's why."

I was sure that this would soon be my fate as well.

Jamen had a cat named Simon that was his constant companion. She was a Siamese cat with blue eyes that adored him. Thankfully, I didn't see her among the carnage.

"Come on. Keep moving," he said, as he shoved me into the house. There was no sound coming from Jamen's room, so with trepidation, I asked, "Where is Jamen?"

"He took off when we got home. He's probably over at Dan's house."

Thank God he got away. I was ushered into the living room and thrust onto the couch. He shoved me so hard that I thought the couch was going to break from the force of the impact. He yelled, "You bitch. You fucking bitch! How could you do this to me?" Then *BAM!* With his fist, I caught the first blow to my arm. *BAM!* came the next blow on the side of my neck. The rampage went on for hours. I sat quietly, afraid to breathe or move.

Silently, I prayed, "Lord, I need you! Please help me! I need to stay alive for my boys." I repeated this simple prayer over and over.

I kept my head down, so as not to defy him. Each time he came close, I would suffer another blow. With the butt of the gun, he was breaking everything. Glass flew everywhere when he struck the stove window. He went on to the storage shelves, destroying them, then the kitchen table. I sat numbly, knowing that my turn was coming.

He rammed the barrel of the gun into my chest while yelling, "You think you can run away from me and take *my* kids?" I sat frozen with fear. *Jesus, please help me!* I silently pleaded; I wasn't going to give Bob the satisfaction of crying out. *Stay strong. Don't let him see your fear.*

He pulled the rifle back and thrust it as if to impale me with it. I closed my eyes bracing for the impact. The barrel went under the crook of my arm, through the couch, and through the wall of our trailer, coming out the other side of the wall. It was not by chance that the barrel had missed me; God had deflected the gun. For the moment, I breathed a sigh of relief. I know that God was right by my side through this whole ordeal, keeping me calm, quiet, and most importantly, alive, although many times throughout the night, I wondered if that would be the outcome.

Through the long night, Bob screamed, "We are both going to die, and the boys will become wards of the state! How would you like that?"

At 11:00 P.M., a patrol car pulled up, shining its lights on the house. From the window, we saw two deputies exit the car and approach the door. Bob quickly shut off the lights and ordered, "Be quiet." He then said, "This is it. We are all going to die, including those two officers, all because of you."

I calmly whispered, "I can get rid of them. It doesn't have to end up this way."

He thought for a moment. "Fine, go on then. Get rid of them," he said.

I cautiously walked past where he was standing and went down the narrow hallway, standing back from the door. Neither the officers nor I could see each other.

Bob fixed the rifle on me. I was to get the first bullet if I failed to get rid of them.

Bam—Bam—Bam. The officer nearest to the door spoke loudly through the closed window. "Ma'am, we got a call about finding your vehicle and we're checking to see if you're alright."

Lord, I need to sound convincing. "My car broke down in the country. I made it home, though, and I'm fine. Thank you for checking on me." *Please Lord, please get rid of them!* They didn't seem to buy my story. *Why should they believe me? The lights are off, and I'm not opening the door to them. They're not stupid, but Lord, I need them to go away. Please send them away.*

The officers talked quietly between themselves for a while, "Well, alright then. If you're sure that you're fine," one of them said and they reluctantly left. *Thank you, God!*

Bob ordered, "Get back to the couch and sit down." Peeking through the window he said, "Watch this. They'll park down by the tree line and discuss this," which is exactly what they did. After about ten minutes they moved on, and I was once again alone.

Bob was taunting me now, but he caught me off guard when he said, "I tell you what. You can take the first shot at me and then I get to take a shot at you. How does that sound?" *He knew about the handgun in my pocket!*

"It doesn't sound very much in my favor," I replied.

After punching me several more times, Bob yelled, "Do you want to be with your mother?"

By that point, any hope of being saved was gone. *If you're going to kill me then just go ahead and do it.*

For the first time that night, I stood boldly and spoke clearly, saying, "Yes, I would rather be with my mother than be here with you!" Releasing his grip on the rifle, it suddenly dropped to the floor. Bob slumped down in the chair and openly wept. I wonder if he felt that he had lost his control over me and given up. The ordeal was over for the time being, and it was difficult not to go over and try to console this sobbing man.

Maureen had been waiting for me at the rental house, but as we never showed, she drove by my house to see if I had changed my mind. Seeing that the van was gone, she headed to her father's golf course just a half-mile away from our house to discuss the situation with him. The two officers went there also to discuss what they had encountered at my home. Since Maureen knew about the situation, she was able to fill them in on the missing pieces to the story. The deputies said, "There is really nothing that we can do. Mrs. Lang acknowledged to us that she was fine and refused our help. We had no choice but to leave."

"But she could be in danger," Maureen replied.

"I'm sorry, but our hands are tied. She said that she was fine. We have another call to attend to."

Jamen came home the following day. He ran, looking for his precious Simon but couldn't find her. Bob didn't say anything to Jamen about running away; he was a broken man at that point. I didn't have to explain to Jamen what had happened the night before. He could see the bruises for himself.

"What happened when Daddy took you home? Did he hurt you?" I asked Jamen.

He focused on the ground, "No, Daddy was calm when he drove me home. He didn't say a word. When we got to the house, I saw that all the cats were dead. Why did he shoot all the cats, Mom?"

"He was mad at me and took it out on them. I'm so sorry, Jamen," I said, as I gently stroked his face. "What happened after you got home?"

"He took me in the house and sent me to my room. Then he sat down at the kitchen table and read the paper," Jamen said.

"How did you end up at Dan's house?" I asked.

"After awhile, I peeked out of my door. I saw that Daddy was still reading, so I snuck down the hallway and out the back door. I crawled under the window so that I wasn't seen. Then I ran through the field over to Dan's house," Jamen explained.

"What took so long to call for help?" I asked.

"Dan's family was just leaving for a football game, and I got in with them. When we came home later, we noticed that the van was still gone. We got worried and called the sheriff's department," he said.

For his own protection, I softly said, "Either stay in your room or play outside, but keep away from your father!" Jamen went sadly to his room.

For the next few days, Bob was very quiet. I honestly think he was feeling regret for his actions, but never came out and said so.

Braden was still gone and would be for several more days. I wasn't sure where Braden was, but he later told me that he had driven about 25 miles to his friend Josh's house. He had a motorcycle hidden there, and leaving my car at Josh's house, Braden rode the motorcycle to Gary's house, 120 miles away, and hid for a few more days.

On September 21, Bob discovered Braden's location. He called Gary and said, "Tell Braden its okay for him to come home now."

Later that day, Braden warily came home in the car. Bob was out in the pasture, so I quickly ushered Braden into his room, telling him everything about the previous days. He was furious and grabbed the video camera from my room. It was nice to see that someone wanted to protect me. I needed that.

On the tape, I stated the date and explained what had transpired the past few days. Braden filmed the bruises on both of my upper arms, neck, chest, and behind my ear. Bob was very careful to place a blow where it wouldn't show when clothed, as he had done with Braden. "I'll put the tape in the safety deposit box for safe keeping. We might need it someday," I said.

I was wearing a red tank top that day, which allowed full view of the bruises. Bob scolded me, "Go put a different shirt on." I don't think that he could bear seeing what he had done to me, and he certainly didn't want the boys to see it. I, on the other hand, wanted him to be reminded of what he had done, to be forced to look at it.

The next few months were quite stressful. "When you go somewhere, you will be allowed to take one of the boys, not both. I don't want you trying to run again." Bob would say.

Bob and I fought continually. I couldn't stand the sight of him, let alone to be around him. One night, I went to the couch. The moon was full, and the light was so bright coming in through the window that I couldn't sleep. Babe barked continually, which vibrated on the windows. I gathered my pillow and blanket again, and went into Braden's doorway and slept there. Braden didn't realize I was there.

Bob rose early the next morning and came searching for me. He saw where I was, grabbed me roughly by the hair, dragged me to my feet, and shoved me into the living room. He threw me into the wall and shouted, "You are one sick mother. Have incest with my son, will you?"

I yelled back at him, "I was sleeping in the doorway! Braden was clear across the room and didn't even know I was there. You're the sick one for even thinking something like that!" His delusions were getting worse and driving me farther away. I was in Alcatraz where there was no possible way of escape, surrounded by water that was drowning me.

Braden had lost all respect for his father, and Bob felt like he had lost total control of Braden. He continually called places to have him committed to. He called Boys Town, detention centers, and every place he could think of. The answer was always the same, "Your son has done nothing to warrant this."

I suggested, "Maybe Braden could go live with Gary. He would take good care of him, and maybe it would take some of the stress away from you." *He would at least be safe there.*

Bob wanted Braden to be miserable, though. "What he needs is to be in a strictly controlled environment, like military school, where he would learn discipline and manners!"

Three months went by until Christmas. I wanted to go to my family's celebration, to take their presents to them. Bob agreed to let me go, but told me, "You can take Jamen with you. Braden must remain here."

Braden pleaded with me, "Mom, please don't leave me here alone with him! Please don't go! You know what he's going to do to me the minute that you leave!"

"It will be alright, Braden. He's calmed down now. I'll bring back your Christmas presents from Grandma and Papa," I assured him.

"I don't want Christmas presents! I want you to stay here, or take me with you!" Braden begged.

"Braden, it will be alright," I tried to reassure him and left.

It was so nice to be away from Bob for an entire day. I told Gary all that had been happening, and he was very sympathetic to our plight. He offered, "You need to get away from Bob! You really need to get those boys out of that situation! Come down here and stay if you need to."

I replied, "I really don't see how that's possible at this point. There doesn't seem to be any way of escape. He never lets me leave the house with both boys, and you know what happened the last time I ran." It was a hopeless situation.

When we returned home the following day, Braden yelled, "While you two were off having fun, Daddy has been knocking me around since the moment that you left. Don't ever do that to me again!" Bob was quiet when we left, and I never expected this.

"I'm so sorry, Braden. I didn't know. I promise you that this will never happen again," I said, with a pang of guilt. The Christmas presents that I brought back did little to take away the betrayal that he felt.

The next day, while Bob was standing at the kitchen window drinking coffee in the evening, he noticed a small fire, and then it disappeared.

A little while later, Braden came in the house and Bob detected smoke on his clothes when he walked past. Bob snapped, "What are you doing? Setting the neighbor's ditch on fire?"

Braden said, "I don't know what you're talking about," and continued into his room.

Bob grabbed him before he got to his doorway, "Let's just see about that." He forced him to go outside and get in the truck to go back down to where he had seen the fire. Less than an hour later, Bob returned alone.

I hesitated to ask, "Where's Braden?"

Bob angrily shot back, "He got away from me in the dark."

Braden came home a few hours later and went into his room. Bob grabbed a baseball bat, went into Braden's room, and asked him again, "Just what really happened out there tonight?"

Braden stuck with his story of innocence. Bob yelled, "I've told you before not to lie to me!" With that, he raised the bat.

I was standing in the living room when I heard the bat hit. I stood frozen. *No, God, no.* I then heard Braden say something and knew he was okay. I breathed a sigh of relief.

Bob stormed out of the room and called the county attorney, "Braden set Amen's ditch on fire. I want that boy arrested!" he shouted.

The county attorney called the Amens to get their side of the story.

Mr. Amen told him, "It was nothing really. The fire was very small, and it's out now. No, we don't want to press charges."

Bob flew into a rage. "Everyone takes Braden's side! Why?" he bellowed.

I slipped into Braden's room later to ask him, "Okay, what really happened out there tonight?"

"I had to get away from Dad and decided go out for a walk. Since it was so dark outside, I lit a torch to light the way. It got too close to the dry grass, and the ditch caught fire. I got scared when I saw the fire and took off my jacket to try to put it out. Then I hurried home."

He laughed when he explained how he had escaped from his dad. "Dad was like a maniac! He stopped the truck and got out. Then he lunged at me and was dodging all over trying to catch me. He was too slow, though, and I made my way up to Amen's farm."

Later that night, after we had all gone to bed, Braden jumped out his window and went back to Amen's farm. He told them about the night's events, and they called the police. Bob and I were awakened by someone pounding on the door. When Bob saw that it was the police at the door, he warned me to keep quiet, whispering, "No bat, no bat, do you hear me?" I nodded that I understood. He mumbled under his breath, "Braden must have snuck out."

Bob answered the door, and calmly asked, "What's the problem, officer?"

"Could you please step outside, sir? We had a report that there was a disturbance here. We're just trying to check it out."

One officer stayed outside with him, while the other came in to talk to me.

"Braden told us what happened tonight. I want to hear your side of the story," the officer said.

I couldn't speak. I was too afraid. The frustrated officer then said, "We can't help you if you won't talk to us."

I asked him, "Are you going to be here tomorrow, and the next day, and the next, to protect us? You can't hold him forever, and he *will* come back and kill us. Will you be here then?"

For quite some time, he assured me that we would be protected, "We will immediately take you and the boys to a shelter, and you will be safe there. I promise you that he won't be able to find you."

I reluctantly gave them a statement of what had happened. The other officer hauled Bob in to the sheriff's office to be booked. One officer stayed behind to find the baseball bat. We searched everywhere, but it was never was found.

The police confiscated all nineteen of Bob's guns and took them to be held in the evidence locker. They didn't want him to be released and have access to a gun. The boys and I followed them to the police department, where they photographed Braden's leg where the baseball bat had hit, and filled out the necessary paperwork to file a statement.

EIGHT

Shelter

I will instruct you and teach you in the way you should go; I will guide you with My eye.

—Psalm 32:8

At 11:00 P.M., we followed a police officer to the battered women's shelter in Norfolk, Nebraska. We had left home with only the clothes on our backs and were venturing into the unknown.

A woman who had been in a similar situation checked us in. Boys over the age of sixteen were considered men at the shelter and therefore not allowed. Braden just barely fell under that guideline. Families were to stay together, so we were assigned a clean room with two bunk beds, with access to a community bathroom, kitchen, dining room, and large TV room, each stocked with donated items. We were also given a voucher to go to the Salvation Army to purchase a new pair of clothes.

We were the only family there at the time, which I was thankful for: I needed some time to think and consider our options. *We can't stay here forever. I want to be in my own home, with my own things, but I know it isn't safe there.*

During the day, there were two workers on hand to help us, with everything from relocating to filing for divorce. In the evening, we were there alone. We were free to come and go as we pleased, as long as we were taking safety into consideration. Outgoing phone calls were allowed, except to the abuser. No incoming phone calls were permitted.

We were not allowed to disclose the location of the shelter. Our van was parked in the garage. The doors to the shelter were locked at 10:00 P.M; if we were not back by then, we would not be able to get back in until 8:00 A.M. the following day. The shelter provided the safety and security that the police officers had promised.

Soon after arriving, I went to the bank to clear out the safe deposit box. I grabbed the videotape, and all of our Certificate of Deposits and bonds. I didn't cash them, but I didn't want Bob to either.

Bob was in jail for several days and released on bail. If I thought he was mad when he was arrested, I knew his fury would be amplified to the point of explosion by this point.

We were on our own, my life was turned upside down, and I had no idea where to turn.

I tried to limit our time in public to a minimum. Too many people could recognize us, and I wanted Bob to think that we had left the area. Knowing his first thought would be that I had run to Gary's house, I didn't dare tell him where I was.

A few days into our stay at the shelter, I called my friend Amy to meet me at an out-of-the-way restaurant. I needed some contact with the outside world, and I valued her wisdom. I was so excited to see her pull up that I rushed out to greet her. Hugging me, she asked, "Are you alright?"

"I'm much better now, thanks," I replied.

She confided to me, "I had been praying for God to provide a way out for you. I prayed specifically that Braden would be hurt, but hurt only enough to provide a way of escape for you—which God did!" I thought that was a really strange prayer, but she is a true prayer warrior and God was faithful to answer her according to His will for our lives.

Amy prayed with me for protection, wisdom, and direction. She hugged me once more and sadly said goodbye. I cautiously returned to the safety of the shelter.

On December 31, 1999, we decided to make a move and headed to Salina, Kansas. I don't know why I picked Salina, but maybe because it was far enough away to feel safe but not too far from my family.

On the way to Salina, Braden was driving and he wanted to stop at Bob's parents' farm to tell them goodbye. I warned him, "No Braden! No! It's too dangerous! We don't know where your dad is!" But ignoring my pleas, he ran into the house and, on his way out, grabbed a gun to protect us.

We travelled cautiously, keeping one eye on the rear view mirror. Roughly two hours later, we arrived at the shelter in Salina. I called Gary to assure him that we were safe, but he had news for us: "The State Patrol is looking for you. Bob told them that Braden had stolen a gun. Now every trooper in Nebraska and Kansas will be looking for you." With urgency, he replied," I'm glad to hear that you're alright, but you need to lose that gun!" I was so upset with Braden.

We stayed at the shelter while we explored the area. Nothing seemed right. If we found a good school, the job was missing and the housing was nothing I could afford. I had thought that rural Kansas would be an economical place to live.

We watched the New Year's 2000 celebration on TV at the shelter. There was nothing for us to celebrate. We wondered what the New Year would hold for us.

After a week of searching, we headed back to Nebraska.

The first thing we had to do was turn in this gun. It was worse than a homing device.

We stopped at the sheriff's department where Bob and I used to work and explained the situation. To prove that I was telling the truth, I told him about the tombstone that Bob had purchased ten years earlier. Braden then gave him the directions to its location.

The officer drove out to the farm and asked Bob about it, while we nervously waited at the sheriff's office. The officer checked out our story with Grandma and Bob, and we were free to go.

We returned to the security of the Norfolk shelter, until I could figure out what our next move would be.

It was suggested by our advisor at the shelter that we go to a therapist. The boys did not want to be there; they sat unresponsive, counting the minutes until they could leave. The therapist zeroed in on me, explaining, "Controlling men target weak women like you. You need to make yourself stronger if you don't want to be the target of another controlling man."

"Don't worry, because I never want to see another man as long as I live." I flatly told him. He gave me a knowing smile back.

I did take his advice under consideration and tried to work through that issue. *How do you make yourself stronger?* I thought about my past. *I will never again allow a man to treat me as a doormat.* Abuse is a gradual process that must be stopped at the onset.

We remained in the seclusion of the shelter for several weeks. It was far too dangerous to return to work. My workplace was open to the public, and I would be quite vulnerable. There were glass storefront windows and I would be putting other people's lives in danger. I'm sure that Bob was checking daily to see if I had returned to my job.

The boys had been out of school for a month, but we couldn't continue with this. I obtained their transcripts and enrolled them in school for a short time in Norfolk. I was so afraid that we would be discovered.

I didn't feel safe going back home. We would be far too accessible there. I called Amy about finding a place to live. She asked, "What do you need, and what can you afford?"

"We need a fully furnished house, and I can afford $200 a month for rent," I replied.

"I will start praying right away on this," she said.

She hadn't prayed for more than a few days when she told me, "The house next door to me is fully furnished and can be yours for $200 a month. The owners are snowbirds and will be in Arizona for the winter." I was absolutely amazed at how God listened to her prayers, and I wanted that in my life.

The house was in Meadow Grove, which was the same town that we were originally headed to in September. We gladly accepted the offer and moved in right away. I bought a $30 intercom and put it up between our houses for safety. I had the protection of my friends, and Bob didn't know where we were. The boys were happy to be back with their friends and going back to their old school.

After a few months, Bob's coworkers were working on the power lines by our house. My recognizable van was parked in the driveway. When I saw the utility truck outside the window only feet from my vehicle, I knew that we had been discovered. Fearing that his coworkers would disclose our location, I got a protection order. Bob abided by it for the most part, but I did see him across the field at Braden's district track meet. I was extremely fearful, but he wore a look that made me feel somewhat sorry for him. He appeared to be heavily medicated. Still, I avoided him as much as possible. It calmed my fears a little that I knew a lot of the men there and that they would come to our aid if need be. Braden, however, approached him and spoke with him for a while.

Bob promised Braden, "Things are going to get better. I was even thinking about getting a motorcycle so we could go riding together. Now get out there and win that race!" Braden was encouraged that his dad finally wanted to start being a part of his life. Even so, he was still leery of his dad, keeping in mind all that had happened in the past. He was not to be so quickly convinced of this miraculous change.

Early that summer, I was out for a walk. As I crossed the farm drive just south of our house, I noticed fresh tire tracks and followed them. The tracks stopped even with our front door. There was a line of trees in between where I suspected Bob had been spying on the house, but I would need to catch him in the act.

I went to the dog pound and picked out a little beagle-dachshund mix, and named him Max. We found out that Max was terribly nervous. My reason for getting a dog was to have a dog that barked at intruders, and I had picked out the only dog in the pound that didn't! He was cute, though, and we decided to keep him.

Braden was sound asleep one night when he heard "Pop, pop, pop!" One by one, he felt nine bullets penetrate his body. He felt warm, thick ooze seeping from the wounds. He woke up startled and ran to tell me, "Daddy broke into my room, and unloaded his revolver into my back!" He was pretty shook up as he recalled the horrific nightmare. "This is the only dream that has ever actually 'hurt'," he said. My heart broke that I was unable to protect him.

Bob's court date was quickly approaching. The sheriff's office said that they needed more evidence to put him in jail. Braden's leg never bruised from the bat incident. Amy advised, "Lori, you have to turn in that videotape, or you will live in fear the rest of your life."

"I know," I replied, "but I'm so scared."

"I know you're scared, but it's something that you have to do."

The following day, I talked with my advocate from the Norfolk shelter. I was torn. I didn't want anything bad to happen to Bob, but at the same time, I didn't want to live in fear.

I reluctantly turned the videotape over to the county attorney.

That afternoon, two officers arrested Bob at his workplace, this time taking him in handcuffs. His mom came to the rescue again with the bond money. I could only imagine how angry he was with me for being arrested a second time.

We continued to lay low.

Bob's court date was set for August 1, 2000. We did not attend the court proceedings. I was too afraid to see him, but my advocate from the shelter was there on my behalf. She later told me, "When they played the videotape, Bob hung his head and couldn't watch it. His brother was seated next to him and did watch it, however."

The county attorney spoke on my behalf explaining to the court about the events of that September night when Bob was first arrested. Judge Ensz asked, "What were you thinking when you put a gun to your wife's head?"

"I wasn't," Bob replied.

Bob tried to explain his actions and that he was no longer a threat to us. He told the court, "I deserve punishment and I've gotten punishment—seven months of no contact with my family, which is my own fault. The only way I can redeem myself is to show my sons that I can support them."

His lawyer added, "Mr. Lang admits to long periods of being irritable, tense, and angry. He has been diagnosed with a persistent anxiety disorder. His counselor says that the chances of the behavior recurring are virtually nil. He has since sought help by attending a batterer accountability class."

He continued, "We plead no contest to the Class IV felony charge of terroristic threats, your honor. We hereby request probation, so that Mr. Lang will retain the ability to provide for his family."

After consideration, Judge Ensz replied, "Your family obviously fears you. Some crimes are just too serious to consider probation. One can't overlook the victims of the crime here." He went on to say, "You seem to have a handle on what happened. You can look back and say, 'I was wrong. I did something that was horribly bad.' Not just bad, horribly bad. You are hereby sentenced to six months in county jail, plus court costs, for terroristic threats."

He was escorted immediately from the courtroom to the county jail. I thought that he would get three years and that we could live in peace, but with domestic issues, it's a different story: Most abusers receive only a fine. In this case, Bob was most likely jailed because of threats to the officers, rather than for my abuse.

My legal advocate at the shelter was also the instructor of the batterer accountability class. She told me about Bob's attitude while in the class. "Bob was the worst one of all the men. He constantly berated the other men for their behavior when his case had the greatest degree of violence."

"Knowing Bob and what he has put us all through, it doesn't really surprise me," I callously replied.

I immediately called the prison to be put on the "call list" when a prisoner is released. I certainly didn't want any surprises.

Months later, I was at the courthouse and happened upon one of the officers who had been at my house that September night when Bob had beaten me. He had learned all that had really happened that evening, and earnestly said, "I am so sorry for leaving you in that situation. We had no idea what was going on, and you wouldn't let us in so we had no choice but to leave."

With the utmost sincerity, I replied, "I am so glad that you left. Bob was just waiting for you to step foot through that door, and he was going to kill us all."

Even though the whole situation seemed hopelessly out of control, God was in total control. I wouldn't have been able to live with the guilt if those officers would have been killed and left families behind because of me.

Years later, Braden inspected the .22 caliber pistol that I had concealed in my pocket that September night. "It's a good thing that you didn't take on Dad with this gun, because it doesn't even work. The trigger mechanism on it is all messed up." I felt validated at that moment.

Amy continued to pray with me daily and work with me to depend on God for all of our needs. She explained to me, "Salvation is by faith. Christ died for your sins and paid your debt on the cross. 'I am the way, the truth, and the life; no one comes to the father, but by me.' (John 14:6) All you have to do is believe, and accept Christ as your Savior."

What my mother had tried to teach me finally made sense. I prayed with Amy, "Dear Jesus, I have made such a mess of my life. Please come into my heart and save me. I want to live for you!" Amy hugged me and rejoiced with me. I am no longer confused, and now know for certain that when I die I will spend all eternity in heaven. I also found that, like Amy, God was listening to me and answering my prayers!

I had been away from my job for so long while we were at the shelter that someone else was hired to replace me. I didn't blame them. I was supporting three people, however, and funds were beginning to dwindle. I needed to find a job.

I made a list of everything that I needed, and wanted, in a job. I included the hours that I wanted, the pay that I needed, the type of job I wanted to do, etc. I then brought this list before God and prayed on it daily. Less than a week later, a job meeting every single detail on my list opened up and I was hired at the Battle Creek Mutual Insurance Co.

Why am I always so amazed that the God of the universe would listen to me?! I love the way that my pastor stated it, "God leans down to listen attentively to what you have to say, because He cares about everything that concerns you."

We had no contact with Bob during his incarceration. The boys had no desire to see him.

I knew that if I saw him, Bob would tell me, "I'm so sorry. I've really changed. I want us to be a family again." I didn't trust myself to be strong.

While Bob was in jail, I received a letter from him. It was written in pencil on jail stationary. I was afraid to open it, so I handed it to Amy to read.

She burst out laughing.

What on earth could be so funny?

She read it out loud, "Feed the horse." That was all it said, no signature or anything else. I felt like such a fool.

Bob didn't need to worry about the horse. I had been taking care of the animals and had turned Dusty out into the pasture. One of the times that I had gone home, Jamen's cat Simon was wandering around the yard. I brought her to our rented house, and Jamen was thrilled to see his beloved pet.

I moved back home to the acreage the first week of November 2000. I obtained court orders stating that Bob had to stay away from us and the property when he was released. He signed the papers agreeing to it.

NINE

Fire!

He raises the poor out of the dust, and lifts the needy out of the ash heap . . .
—Psalm 113:7

November 13, 2000, was particularly cold—11 below zero—so frigid that a late start was called for school. I went on to work, leaving the boys to drive in when it was time. School was finally called off because of blizzard conditions.

Around 10:00 A.M., my boss, Vicki, who happened to be a paramedic, yelled, "Lori, your house is on fire!"

I threw on my coat and raced out the door, driving the four miles home in a panic and praying, "Please, dear God, don't let this be happening! Please protect my boys! Please, God, please! Please, help me!"

When I rounded the last corner, the black smoke was so thick that I couldn't see the highway. My heart sank with the realization that this was my home trickling across the road. I saw Braden was standing outside, not wearing a jacket and holding a cell phone. He had shut off the electricity and propane. He even tried to put out the fire with a garden hose, but everything was frozen.

I stood there weeping, watching the flames consuming our home. There was no use trying to save anything. The entire house had been lost in the ten minutes it took me to get home.

Braden wrapped his arms around me and said, "Everything's going to be all right, Mom," It took a moment to come to my senses, when I frantically asked him, "Where is Jamen? I don't see Jamen!"

Braden replied, "He's fine. He took off for Dan's house the minute he heard school was cancelled." Both of my boys were alive and unharmed. *Thank you, God!*

The rural electric company had gotten the call about the fire and sent a truck out to make sure the power was off. They were impressed that Braden had thought of it already. One of the guys removed his jacket and handed it to Braden.

"What on earth happened?" I asked Braden.

"I went out to start the car and let it warm up. Then I heard on the radio that school was called off, so I went out and shut it off. I walked by the window a while later and saw that the car and carport were in flames. I raced to try to put out the fire, but when I opened the door, flames came rushing into the house."

The Battle Creek Fire Department arrived about ten minutes after I did. It's a volunteer department, and all the men have jobs they must quickly abandon before gathering at the fire hall to go out on a call. The Meadow Grove Fire Department also responded.

While watching them work, I noticed that my room had not yet burned and yelled at the firemen, "Go around to the back of the house. Get my bedroom before it catches on fire!" They quickly pulled around to the back and started pumping water right away. Most everything was charred and ruined, but it was contained quickly and I was extremely grateful to both fire departments.

Jamen had seen the fire from Dan's house, and they rushed over to find out what was going on. Jamen frantically said, "Simon! Did Simon make it out?"

Braden shook his head and sadly told him, "No. None of the cats made it out."

Jamen was devastated beyond our ability to console him. Dan put his arm around him and took him back to his house. Braden and I drove to our church to tell the pastor what had happened. I desperately needed a support group at this time.

A group of men were there, volunteering their services to build an addition to the church. When they heard what had happened, they opened their wallets and passed the hat for us. I was overwhelmed by the generosity of strangers. One of the men said, "We passed through the smoke on the highway and wondered what was burning."

"Just my whole life," I replied.

I humbly thanked the men, and we left. Since I had nowhere else to go, I went back to work and Braden went to Josh's house.

When I arrived at my workplace, a Red Cross representative was waiting for me in the break room. I walked down the long hallway through all the women who had gathered to offer consolation. The Red Cross worker handed me a small plastic bag with some necessities in it and a voucher to buy clothes, coats, and shoes. She then said, "The Red Cross will pay for a few nights in a hotel until you can find other arrangements."

"Thank you, but my boys and I need to be close to friends right now," I said.

"I can fully understand that under the circumstances," she gently replied.

Braden made a call to his dad in jail and told him about the fire. Bob assured him, "Everything will be all right. I'm just glad everyone is safe. I'm so glad that you called me." He finished by saying, "I love you, Braden."

"I love you too, Dad," Braden replied as he hung up the phone. Braden longed for that elusive relationship. He needed to hear those comforting words from his dad.

Braden and I returned to the house when the fire was completely out. We despairingly surveyed the tangled mess that lay before us.

The interior walls were gone so we tried to figure out where rooms had been by objects that we found. The washer and dryer, refrigerator, and stove were still in place. I stood back and tried to visualize the rooms. The firemen's hoses were powerful, though, and what should have been in one place was now somewhere else.

There was nothing but a shell left of the car. Sitting next to the car were the remnants of a 1980 Honda motorcycle that Braden had purchased the previous month from his teacher.

Then as I was going through the debris pile, I found the greatest gift of all. All of my photographs had been spared! I could hardly contain my excitement. God had seen to it to spare the most important things to me: my children and my photographs. Since we had just moved back into our house, I had not fully unpacked. Large trash bags full of clothes were piled in the corner of my bedroom, on top of the box of photos, protecting them. Only the edges of the photographs were charred.

If Jamen had been home, he would have tried to save everything, especially Simon. Someone later gave him a Siamese kitten. Recently, I came across the photo that I had taken of the two of them. There is such a haunting sadness in Jamen's eyes. This little ball of fluff was adorable, but it could never replace Simon.

Our friends graciously opened up their homes to us, each of us going to a separate home. I would stay with Amy, Jamen with Dan, and Braden with Josh.

This was all so surreal. I had just begun unpacking our things before the fire. My sole possession was now a small bag from the Red Cross that contained a comb, bar of soap, wash cloth, toothpaste, and toothbrush. I held up the bag to Amy and wailed, "This is all that I own in the whole world! We have no insurance, nothing!" I broke down and wept. Utter despair consumed me.

I pleaded, "Lord, what am I going to do? Where am I going to go?"

Amy ran to her bedroom and grabbed her Bible. She sat beside me at the kitchen table and read God's promises to me. She read a passage from Joel stating, "I will replace what the locusts have eaten," and also "what the fire has destroyed." (Joel 2:25) She kept reassuring me, "It will be alright, Lori. Our God is faithful and just! This did not slip through His fingers. He does have a plan in all of this."

"I want to believe you Amy, but I really feel like I'm being punished right now," I cried.

"God isn't punishing you," she reassured me. "He loves you and will turn this tragedy around for good. His plans are to prosper you and not harm you. His Word assures us of that, even when everything looks bleak right now."

The following day, the flood gates opened. Bags of clothes were showing up by the truckload. Where we previously had twenty-year-old things, we were now receiving new things. I was overwhelmed by the outpouring of kindness toward us.

A kind man purchased a trailer house for us. Another man gave us a car. God kept blessing us every time we turned around. It was extremely humbling to witness firsthand the love and concern of our neighbors. After I lost everything I owned, I realized that possessions just didn't matter like they once did. "Do not store up for yourselves treasures on earth, where thieves break in and steal. But store up for yourselves treasures in heaven, where moth and rust do not destroy." (Mathew 6:19-20)

During my stay with Amy, she patiently worked with me. These were my first real steps heading back to God. Even though He had been with me the whole time, I had not made time to have a personal relationship with Him. I had not really allowed Him to be a part of my life. I had been living as the master of my destiny, but look where that had gotten me.

We would not be able to get the new trailer in place until spring. The water, gas, and sewer lines needed to be retrenched and repaired first, and that couldn't be accomplished until the ground thawed. So we waited for warmer weather.

In Battle Creek, Red Bud Hardware set up a table for us. We were asked what we needed, and someone would purchase it. The owner called me in several times to put more requests for items on the table because everything had been purchased. It was quite a humbling experience. The townspeople then had a "shower" for us and presented us with all the wonderful gifts. They were truly a blessing from God.

One day when I was in Red Bud, a woman that I didn't know came up to me and placed $20 in my hand. It is so heartwarming to see the genuine love and concern of this tight knit community.

The Meadow Grove Fire Department held a benefit for us at the fire hall. People poured in all morning. So many of these people didn't know who we were, but they opened their hearts to us anyway. I can never thank these fine people enough.

In the next few weeks, Amy helped me with the daunting task of sifting through the rubble. Everything was the same color: black. Most things had changed in shape and form. Things had melted together, which made the task that much more difficult.

I was looking for a very special ring that my mother had given to me when she died. It had five diamonds, one for her, and four others to represent her children. We uncovered other jewelry that survived, but we never found that ring.

We did, however, find every Q-tip that we had ever owned. They must be virtually indestructible. Of all the things we could afford to lose, I think those were it. Their discovery did spur a moment of laughter between us, which we desperately needed at the moment.

The fire was so fast; it had raced through the flimsy trailer without the intense heat developing like you would have with a house fire. The hopes of finding my rings unscathed seemed high. We found pieces of Braden's prized steam shovel. I uncovered a charred fragment of the sweater that my mother had painstakingly made for me. Each new find brought back so many memories and heartache all over again.

Had I known that our house would be gone that fateful day, I would have definitely chosen a different outfit to wear. I would have worn my favorite blue jeans and tennis shoes. Instead, I dressed to keep warm from the extreme cold. I never left the house without a necklace and my rings on, but that day I forgot them all. *Why that day, of all days?*

The black soot filled my lungs, ears, hair, and between my toes. I was so tired of being dirty, but I needed to keep searching in case there was something that had possibly been spared.

Friends came to help with the cleanup. My friend, Tammy, arrived with a tractor to move piles of mangled and twisted debris. I gently combed the piles of rubble with a small hand rake, to see if any treasures could be uncovered. Coins, wrestling medals, and trinkets that the boys made in school began to materialize. I held each item adoringly in my hand, like I was on an archeological dig and had just found a precious artifact.

Our friend, Bill, showed up with a torch and cut the trailer beams into manageable pieces that could be moved. Others came to help us search in the freezing cold for anything that could be salvaged. Sadly, there wasn't much left.

I needed to have the debris removed from the site to make way for our new trailer. With no means to accomplish that task myself, I made a few calls for quotes. I decided to place an ad in the paper, "Give-away: scrap metal, you haul." Within one week, I received eight calls from people who would take it. Within a few days, all of the rubble had been removed at no cost.

Now began the process of starting over. We moved back into the house that we had just left in Meadow Grove and waited for spring. Due to the circumstances, the owner said that we could stay there at no charge for as long as we needed to.

I couldn't understand why all of this had happened. We weren't bad people, so why did bad things keep happening to us?

On December 3, 2000, I received a phone call saying, "This is the Prison Vine. This is to inform you that inmate Robert Lang has been released from the Madison County Jail as of this date." I wasn't expecting the call so soon. I thought that he had two months left to serve.

Fear and panic suddenly overtook me. I wanted to disappear.

We stayed hidden that day at our house in Meadow Grove. I suspected that he would go home to survey the damage and then would head south to his parent's home in Geneva.

TEN

Don't Come Any Closer . . .

Fear not, for I am with you; be not dismayed, for I am your God. I will strengthen you, Yes, I will help you, I will uphold you with my victorious right hand.

—Isaiah 41:10

December 7, 2000, was to be a beautiful day, with a high of 50 degrees. I went to work, but my thoughts were on getting out to the debris pile. I was there whenever weather permitted and today was a perfect day to search.

I had made plans to leave work at 11:00 A.M., but there were still many phone calls coming in from concerned friends, which were taking me away from my work. My boss was becoming increasingly aggravated with me. He finally stopped by my desk at 10:30 A.M., and said, "Lori, you are not being paid to sit on the phone with noncustomers. Now, get back to work!" I didn't want to upset him any further and decided that I would stay at work instead. At 3:20 P.M., I picked Jamen up from school and we drove out to the burn site. Braden had a car and would meet us there.

When we arrived, the yard was full of cars that I didn't recognize, and a lot of people were milling around. *What on earth is going on? Did a hunter come on the place and get hurt?*

While scanning the cars, I spotted a familiar one and recalled it belonging to Bob's parents. I looked down on the ground next to the car and found that I was viewing a familiar scene from too many TV shows: where there is a person lying on the ground covered by a sheet, with only their boots showing.

Oh my gosh! NO! I recognized the boots as Bob's.

At the dreaded realization of what I was seeing, my heart sank. Jamen and I stood there, numbly watching, when several men rushed to my van warning me, "Don't come any closer!" I reached out for Jamen's hand.

One of the men, the county attorney, recognized me and gently said, "I am so sorry to have to tell you this, but Bob used a shotgun and took his life." I couldn't believe what I was hearing. He went on to explain, "Your neighbor, Kelvin, found a suicide note in his mailbox. The note simply stated that Bob was going to take his life and where he could be found."

I was playing this all out in my mind, trying to comprehend what he was saying to me. Kelvin seemed quite shaken as he stood talking with Braden, recalling the events that led up to this. I felt terribly sorry for him.

There was definitely an intervention by God in this. Had Kelvin not checked his mail, he wouldn't have known about Bob's death. The boys and I would have gone out there as planned, and we would have been the ones to find him instead. I'm so thankful that the boys didn't have to live with that horrible memory.

There will always be many unanswered questions, but strangely I felt a sense of relief. I would not have to live in fear.

I felt cold and calloused, like I was dead inside.

The county attorney suggested, "You really should take the boys and leave. You don't want to see any of this. The sight is pretty gruesome. It's really best if you don't return for a few days, so that nature can take its course." I mulled over those awful words in my head, wanting to erase the images that I knew he was implying.

None of us said anything. We kept our eyes fixed on the white sheet, deep in our own thoughts.

I had a car appointment later that day. When we were told to leave my property, I didn't know what else to do but to keep the appointment and have the car repaired. So much had happened that I was totally incapable of decision, or of feeling any emotion. Years later, I read about acute stress reaction brought on by a traumatic situation. It said, "There is an initial state of 'daze,' which happens within minutes of the event. Withdrawal from the surrounding situation may occur, to the extent of a dissociative stupor." That summed up what we were going through at that particular time.

The police had hauled Bob's parents' car off to be impounded. It was not involved in a crime, so this decision was confusing and frustrating. The cost to hold the car was mounting day by day. Not wanting his parents to have a massive bill to get their own car back, the boys and I drove to Norfolk to retrieve it.

When we arrived, I paid the $150 fee and was handed the keys in return. We located the car in the lot, and I climbed into the front seat. My attention was drawn immediately to a check made out to me, lying on the seat. The check was for $1,300 to close out Bob's checking account. Next to the check lay Bob's glasses. I picked them up, and overwhelming sadness hit me. I don't know why seeing his glasses had such an impact on me, possibly because they brought some of his final moments to light. I tried to piece together in my mind the events that had led up to that fateful moment and, just as quickly, I shook my head to erase them.

In the passenger's seat lay a Bible, which stunned me. Bob was not one to have a Bible in his possession. I opened up the cover for any clues as to where it came from. It was inscribed,

"*To Robert,*

Blessings from Northern Heights Baptist Church," and was signed, "*Pastor Steve.*"

Questions raced through my mind. *Had Bob been attending this church? Did Pastor Steve mentor him in jail? Did Bob accept Christ as his Savior?*

My attention turned back to the task at hand. I turned the key to start the car, and a Christian radio station came on. I wondered what all had gone through his mind in those final moments. How hard it must have been. I tried not to visualize his last moments, but those thoughts wouldn't leave me alone. It would haunt me for a long time.

In the back seat, I found several partially burned marriage books that he had purchased for me, on how to be a better wife. I felt like he was telling me, "See, you should have been a better wife, and this wouldn't have happened."

In the car was also a note that he had written. It read, "No more counseling, no more pain, no more being separated from my family." It looked like he was trying to justify what he was about to do. It was hard to read the desperation coming from him near the end.

One thing I noticed is that on his final day on earth, he reached out to God. I genuinely hoped that he found Him that day and was ready to go home. I pray that he asked Jesus to save him right then and there. I was encouraged by the two signs that were left for us to find: the radio station and the Bible. It gives me great hope to believe that I will see him again someday. I would look forward to that, because all of the bad would be removed and only the good in him would remain.

"God, why didn't you allow him to die in a car accident on the way up here instead? It would have been much easier for us to handle. We wouldn't be tortured with all the 'if only' . . . and 'why' questions had that been the case. I just don't understand God!" I prayed.

A wise friend suggested, "Maybe God needed those final moments for Bob to accept Him. Had he died in an accident before then, he might have missed that chance." I sincerely hope that was the case.

I could see God's protection for me being revealed. I heard later from a neighbor that he had seen Bob standing in front of our burned home at 1:00 P.M. Had I not stayed at work, I would have been there at that exact time, also. There would have been no protection for me.

God knew what Bob's plans were and also what I was planning. Thankfully, He used my boss to intervene, which is something I didn't appreciate at the time. My boss apologized to me the next time that I was at work, "I'm so sorry that I got upset with you, Lori. I didn't know about any of this."

I earnestly replied, "God used you, to get mad at me, to keep me at work. You might have saved my life. I can never thank you enough!"

I believe in my heart that the fire happened for a reason. Bob had no home to return to. Nothing in the home was his to claim. I also believe it was to provide a "way out" for us. Losing our home seemed to be the only way.

We had all lived through my greatest fear, and everything was going to be alright. God never paces the halls wondering what to do. He is always in total control even when we can't see what He is doing.

The week after Bob died, I had six offers to buy my land. People were coming out to the property when we were sifting through the rubble. They also came to my workplace, saying, "You will never be able to go back there and live, there are too many memories. You should just sell it." It was rather upsetting to me. It was a beautiful acreage in a great location, and I loved it there. *This is my home.* I wanted to be around something familiar, to bring some sense of normalcy back to our lives. It was never a question to sell it. I was quite vulnerable at this particular time and didn't want to make any rash decisions.

Amy went with me to the funeral home to make the final arrangements. We walked up a long flight of stairs and were ushered into a sitting room.

A nice man helped us get through all the paperwork. Since Bob and I had discussed our final wishes many times, I knew what he wanted, which made it much easier.

The mortician said, "We need to write up an obituary for the paper." He cautiously continued, "We will have to include the fact that it was a suicide."

Why was that detail so important? *Let him die with some dignity and respect.*

The obituary read, "Memorial services for Robert R Lang, age 44, will be Tuesday, December 12th at 4:30 p.m. at the First United Methodist Church in Battle Creek. There will be no visitation, and internment will be at a later date. He died Thursday, December 7, 2000, of an apparent suicide."

While we were at the funeral home, I asked, "Is Bob here?"

The man helping us replied, "Yes, he's in the next room, but you don't want to see him." It seemed odd to think that he was in the same building with us. I was fighting the ghastly pictures that were filling my mind. I recalled as a child sneaking into my dad's forbidden trunk and seeing those gruesome images. I didn't want to think of Bob that way. I wanted to get out of there.

Bob did not want to be embalmed, under any circumstance. He had seen it done too many times when he was a cop, and he didn't want that for himself. When I noticed a charge for embalming on the bill, I emphatically explained Bob's views on the matter to the mortician. He gently replied, "It's too late, I'm afraid it's already been done. I'm really sorry. We will be sure to remove the charge from your bill."

I was distraught that I was unable to accommodate Bob's wishes.

The funeral director sent me directly to the Social Security Office with the death certificate. "This will enable you to get the boys lined up for monthly social security checks. You will also receive a $250 check, as a death benefit, to help with burial costs," he said.

It was comforting to know that I would be able to support the boys. I remember sitting in that office when a strange realization hit me. *I am now a widow.* I felt almost like part of my identity had suddenly been stripped away.

The next day, I got out of bed and looked out the window. The sun was just starting to come up. As I watched it, I thought to myself, *Hmmm, the sun does still continue to rise. The world still goes on as usual, even though my world has changed.* My life would never be the same; I would have to find a new "normal." But the world still turns and barely even notices.

Not knowing what else to do, I sent the boys to school and I returned to work. I would come to regret the decision to send the boys to school that day. I had no idea that the school was going to announce the entire incident over the intercom. They even included the part about the note left in the mailbox.

The boys said, "We were just sitting there at our desks, when they started announcing everything, and then everyone just turned and stared at us. It was so humiliating, Mom."

Amy was aghast when her kindergarten-age daughter came home and told her about it.

I was so angry when I called the school and suggested, "If this situation ever comes up again, it should definitely be handled differently!"

The principal replied, "I'm sorry, but we wanted to squelch all of the rumors at the start, so the kids could concentrate on their school work."

"I really have to disagree. All that was accomplished was giving the kids more to talk about. There should have been a better way to handle this. My kids have been through enough and didn't need to be humiliated on top of it. Please see to it that this never happens again," I said, as I hung up the phone.

Two days later, the funeral home called, "The cremation has been done. You may come and pick up the urn at any time." I drove over after work. I was shocked when the mortician handed me a black plastic box, the size of a shoebox, with a label reading "Robert Lang" on it.

"I was expecting something much larger," I replied. I reluctantly took the box from him. *This is my husband! A few days ago he was alive and well, and going on with life as usual, and now this.*

I was so angry with Bob at that moment! It was such an incredible waste. *It didn't have to be this way! You had so much to offer! Why did you have to do this?* I warily set Bob in the front seat of the van and left. The whole way home I kept looking at the black box in stunned silence.

The boys were speechless when I got home and showed them the urn. This brought harsh reality to light.

We did not have the money to pay for a funeral, so we decided to conduct the service ourselves. We asked people from our church to lead the music and for our pastor to perform the service. We printed up bulletins and song sheets. The church was beautifully decorated for a celebration, not a funeral. Garland festively adorned two Christmas trees. The urn was placed on a small table near the podium, and was covered by a lace tablecloth.

Bob's coworkers came to the service dressed in their uniforms as a tribute to Bob. Not as many people showed up as I had expected. In retrospect, the situation was rather awkward and no one knew quite how to grieve, or what to say.

When I turned around in the pew, I thought that I caught a glimpse of Bob's brother in the back row. He quickly slipped out before the service ended, however, so I never had the chance to speak with him.

After the service, the pastor commented to me, "I was watching the boys, and I have never conducted a funeral service in which the kids didn't shed a tear, until now." I know that I didn't cry either, which I'm sure didn't go unnoticed.

We received one sympathy card. The details leading up to this had circulated through town, and I think people weren't sure if a card was appropriate or not.

When Bob resigned from work, he lost his benefits along with his life insurance. We used most of the money from the fireman's benefit for the cremation and funeral.

Bob had told me, "I could never kill myself. I've seen too many botched suicides. I would never take the chance on being an invalid." It's sad that he felt that this was the only alternative.

Being a convicted felon was probably a contributing factor. He would probably have found it difficult to find a job. He had lost his family and his home. Respect is vital to a man, and he had lost the respect of the town and us.

A few weeks after his death, I received the nicest card in the mail from the funeral director. It stated, "I would like to help you with the recovery efforts from the fire and your husband's death. I hope that this helps." He included a check for $1,000 from his own personal account. This money could be used for so much!

The nightmare of dealing with Bob's estate began. I was still his wife, but my name was omitted from everything. I thought that my name was on all of the accounts, but I was wrong. I had to pay over $1,000 to a legal firm to get back what was mine to begin with. It was all quite frustrating, and it was a lot of money that I couldn't afford at the time.

We had a large sum of money in the bank, with the hopes of building a house someday. I would need this money to rebuild our lives now. When I contacted the bank, we were advised that Bob had beaten us to it. He had told them, "I want to cash out all of my Certificates of Deposit. I lost the originals, however. Will that be a problem?"

After pulling up the account, the clerk replied, "No problem, sir. I see that they all say, 'Robert &/or Lori.' So they don't require both signatures, only one. And since they were lost, we don't need the originals. We have copies of them here."

He easily cashed out $50,000 that I had thought was safe in my possession. *How can this keep happening to me? Is there no end to this terrible dream? I have to find that money!*

Maybe Bob gave it to one of his family members for safe keeping? I wrote a letter to his mother inquiring about it. She mailed me back a letter that Bob had written while in jail. The letter was dated November 13, 2000, and said, "Braden called and said that the house burned today. Along with it, I had $54,000 in a shoebox in the tool room, which also burned." I recognized his handwriting but had a hard time believing what he wrote. The word "tool room" appeared to have been erased and written over, so I questioned if the money had been there at all.

Christmas of 2000 was extremely hard. Bob was gone, our home was gone, and everything we owned was gone. Even my mother was not here for guidance and support. The mood was very somber.

While we were at the store using our Red Cross voucher, I ran into a friend named Laurie who was talking to a tall, handsome man.

She reached out and hugged me, saying, "Oh, Lori, I'm so sorry to hear about everything you have been going through."

"God has been doing some amazing things for us. He provided a house with everything we needed to get by, and the people of Battle Creek have been wonderful in helping us," I replied. Showing her the voucher, I said, "Look, we even have money from the Red Cross to buy new clothes."

"I'm so glad to hear that. It was great seeing you!" she exclaimed.

"You too, Laurie," I replied. "Have a Merry Christmas!"

I heard later that Laurie had explained our situation to this man who happened to be a local radio station manager. He was there giving away a $5000 shopping spree to a somewhat ungrateful recipient. I was told that he had wished that we were the winners instead.

A week later, I was overwhelmed to receive a large box full of gifts from the radio station. I slumped to the floor and cried.

We took the box of gifts to Gary's house for our Christmas celebration. They were the only gifts that year, which made them even more special. There was a remote-control hummer, CDs to replace Braden's music that was lost, games for the boys, and all sorts of wonderful things. It was incredibly heartwarming that someone would show such kindness to us. I prayed, "Lord, please heap great rewards upon this kind gentleman who thought of us."

The box containing Bob's ashes was still in the van when we went down to the family Christmas. Braden commented, "You know, this is the only Christmas I can remember where all four of us were together and all getting along."

I sadly admitted, "You're right. It is."

Our silent passenger would accompany us for the next two years. We didn't know what to do with the ashes, and so they remained in the van after the funeral.

A few weeks after Christmas, I received a call from a deputy stating, "We have Robert Lang's personal effects being held at our office. You are welcome to pick them up at any time." The boys and I promptly drove to the sheriff's department in Madison, Nebraska.

When I walked into the office, I was handed Bob's wallet and other personal items. I clutched them to my chest. In his wallet was a receipt from Country Kitchen dated December 3, 2000, at 10:00 A.M. He had ordered a large breakfast, most likely relishing a good full meal for the first time in months. It was sad to think that the contents of his wallet revealed the last fragments of his life.

The boys wanted mementos of their father. One took his driver's license, while the other took his diploma card.

In June of 2001, I heard that a State Patrol trainee had been riding along with an officer the day Bob died. It was his first day out and his first call. When he arrived at the scene, he was horrified and sickened by what he saw.

He went home and told his wife, "I'm not cut out for this line of work. I'm looking into another career."

"I'm so glad! I never wanted to be married to a cop," she exclaimed.

It is amazing how many lives are affected by decisions that we make, knowingly or not.

The guilt of Bob's death was overwhelming. *This was all my fault!* Every night for over a year, I cried myself to sleep. *If only I had been a more loving wife. If only I had not left him. If only I had not turned the videotape in, he would still be alive.*

I was tormented by the "what ifs" and "whys." *This should never have happened. He didn't need to die. He could've been a good man. He was funny and intelligent, with so much to offer the world.*

Like everyone else, he just wanted to be loved. I had such a hard time giving him that love, though. It is so hard to love someone, and not like them at the same time. His illness could have been controlled so easily. It's frustrating that our lives were so miserable when medication could have changed all of that. So many wasted years! I had seen his good side and wished so much that the good man would have come home every night instead of the hurtful one.

What didn't help with my guilt was the fact that Bob's parents and brother blamed us for his death.

Bob had told me, "When I die, I want my ashes spread around the oak tree on my parents' farm." I should have granted his final wish but didn't feel that we were very welcome at the farm to accomplish it.

On Braden's sixteenth birthday, he received a card from his grandmother stating, "If you ever come around here again, I will have you arrested. Enjoy your birthday." He was devastated to read the angry words. He had spent four years of his childhood being raised by them, and they had been very close. I regretted not opening the card before I handed it to him. I would have thrown it away if I had.

Thankfully, years down the road, Braden's relationship with his grandparents was restored.

Suicide is an easy way out, but it also cheats the people who love you. Bob's parents were cheated out of a son, his siblings were cheated out of a brother, and the boys out of a father.

When you are a child, a parent has authority over you and you are on two different levels. As the child grows, the two separate levels come closer together. The two are more on equal terms as the child becomes an adult, thus having more of a friend-friend relationship than a parent-child relationship. Sadly, my boys never got the chance to have that friendship with their father, which I believe could have been possible someday.

Bob's coworkers were stunned to hear what had actually been happening at home. He was always so much fun and kept the morale at work high. He had hoped to be a manager of a company someday and had even returned to school taking night classes to accomplish his goal, and was on the president's list for excellent grades.

One of Bob's coworkers, Matt, said to me one day, "You know, I never realized this until just now. All the other guys would vent at work when they weren't happy with how something was being done. Not Bob, though. He would just go along with it and keep his mouth shut. While the other guys fumed and vented, he kept it all bottled up inside."

"That was until he got home," I replied. "Then he felt free to vent, and take it out on us."

"It all kind of makes sense now," Matt responded.

I remember a *Good Housekeeping magazine* series entitled, "Can This Marriage Be Saved?" I pondered that question. I honestly believe if we would have had God at the center of our marriage, the answer would have definitely been "yes." I have seen God work miracles in hopeless marriages many times before.

Am I advising a woman to stay with an abusive husband? Absolutely not! If a woman is in a dangerous situation, she definitely needs to get out but with the hope of reconciliation. Bob had no reason to change while I remained there. Everything was just as he wanted it to be. In order for God to work on Bob's heart, I needed to be somewhere safe and out of the way. Bob refused to take responsibility for his actions. It was easier to place the blame on me. If an abuser refuses to repent and seek help, there is no hope for restoration. I was not responsible for the abuse, but as long as I was there, he would continue the abuse.

I wasn't going to file for divorce when we ran. I had no reason to. All I needed at that time was to protect my family. Things just spiraled out of control from there.

Since Bob's case was now closed, his guns were being released by the sheriff's department. The boys and I drove to Madison to pick up the guns from the evidence locker. When we arrived, the attending officer said, "I'm sorry. Your husband's brother contacted us recently and said that all of the guns were his. So, I can't release them to you."

"My husband purchased all nineteen of those guns while we were married," I responded with a hint of frustration. "You took them out of our gun case, which I showed you."

"I'm sorry, but without a court order, I can't release them to you," he replied.

All of our paperwork had burned in the fire, so once again, I hired a lawyer to obtain what was ours. After a long battle, the court finally released them to me and we promptly sold them all.

ELEVEN

A New Normal

The Lord is my helper; I will not fear. What can man do to me?
—Hebrews 13:6

Yet the Lord longs to be gracious to you; he rises to show you compassion. For the Lord is a God of Justice.
—Isaiah 30:18

The boys and I gathered things around the property that could be salvaged or sold. Bob had purchased a pile of trailer axles earlier at an auction. We also had a truck bed trailer. I had no use for them, and we needed the money. I printed up flyers and posted them around town.

One afternoon, I was sifting through the debris pile when a large man drove up in a newer black Dodge pickup.

"I came to see the axles that were on the flyer," he said. He gestured toward the carnage. "What on earth happened here?"

"Our house burned down, and my husband took his life a few days ago. Things are pretty tough right now, so I'm trying to sell some things."

I led him to where the axles were being stored.

"They appear to be just what I need. I'll take all of them. I do need to get my trailer in the morning, and then I'll pick them up around 10:00 A.M. I can bring along a check for $1,000 at that time. Does that work for you?" he asked.

"That sounds just fine; I'll see you tomorrow morning then," I replied.

The boys and I were there by 10:00 A.M. the following day only to see that all of the axles and our truck bed trailer were gone!

I was aghast that someone could have the audacity to steal from a widow and her children, when he had just seen them searching through the rubble of their burned home. *What kind of a person does that?*

I was so furious for months, praying for God to heap justice on this deplorable man! Finally, though, I decided that I had to forgive him and to turn the matter over to God. I'm sure that God dealt swiftly with the situation. I found myself feeling sorry for this man.

Spring finally arrived, and we were able to get the trenching for the water and gas hookups done. Next, we moved the new trailer in. There were no steps that came with the trailer, so the electricians working on the house set up a ladder. I was using the ladder to move large boxes of possessions into the house. I carefully stepped on each rung of the ladder, but I must have missed one because the box and I went crashing to the ground. When I tried to stand up, I found that I couldn't put any weight on my ankle.

Braden helped me limp to the car and drove me to the doctor who found a fractured bone in my ankle. *Great, just what I need right now!* I was given a green cast and provided with crutches.

"Do not put any weight on it for several weeks," the doctor advised. *He obviously doesn't know that we are in the process of moving.*

We still managed to get moved into our trailer, just a little slower.

My coworkers were always anxious to see what disaster I had incurred over the weekend. I never seemed to let them down. The saga just seemed to go on and on. My boss told me, "You really need to write a book, because truth is definitely stranger than fiction when it comes to your life." I was beginning to believe that by now.

The trailer was in place, and I hired two men to tie it down and level it. I told them, "Please use the existing anchors, which are still stuck firmly in the ground" showing them where they were located under the trailer. I went on to explain, "My husband had used the longest anchors that he could find, since we are situated on a sand pile." Nebraska is subject to high winds, and Bob had taken the precaution to make sure that the trailer would stand firm under those conditions.

I had purchased two truckloads of cement blocks that would be used to jack the trailer up. After several hours of work, the job was completed. I paid the $800 requested, and the men left.

Four days later, at around 11:00 P.M., our home was hit by a 70-plus MPH wind. I thought for sure we were going to lose our home. The trailer rocked wildly with every new blast. It sounded like the siding was going to be ripped clean off.

Do we try to run? It's not safe to be out in a car in this wind, either, and where would we run to?

I was so fearful that I knelt beside my bed, and pleaded, "Dear God, please protect my family and our new home that You have given to us. I'm really scared! Please help us, Lord!"

Finally at peace, I went back to bed, trusting God that we would be fine. A half hour later, the fierce winds picked up the end of the trailer, lifting it in the air. Again I screamed, "God, please help us!"

I was so scared and thought for sure that we were going over. I could feel myself floating, and then with a "thump," I hit my bed. My end of the house had lifted up, moved over a few feet, and came crashing back down. I ran down the hall and urgently told Braden, "Go outside and move the cars away from the house in case the trailer goes over, so that we don't lose those, too!" He ran out and did as he was told.

We huddled together in the living room to wait out the storm.

An hour or so later, the winds finally calmed and the storm moved on. "Thank you Lord, for Your protection," I prayed.

The following day, we went outside to survey the damage. Not one block that the men had laid was still in place. I then discovered that they had used flimsy anchors, not the ones that I had requested. "How hard would it have been to tie into the existing anchors?" I fumed.

Thankfully, the trailer had not been moved far enough to damage any of the pipes, which all bent with it. I angrily contacted the men hired to level the trailer and relayed what had taken place.

"Sorry, it's not my problem, lady. But for another $800, I'll come back and fix it," he replied.

I hotly responded, "I will be speaking to my lawyer!"

He stuck by his statement. Braden said, "Forget about this guy. I'll do it myself, and I'll do it right this time."

Braden went under the house and worked in the soot all day, jacking the trailer back up and restacking blocks. He didn't wear a mask, so he was breathing in the thick soot that he was stirring up. He developed bronchitis and was prescribed an inhaler.

Braden was a hurdler in track and was favored to go to the state competition that year. He was coughing so badly during the qualifying meet that he barely won the race that awarded him a spot on the state track team. As one of the faster runners in the state, he was expected to do well and bring home a medal. He ran at State, but the bronchitis would not allow him to do his best. Sadly, he came home empty handed.

Months later, I came home from work and was struck by a wave of fear. Bob was standing on my doorstep! My breathing grew heavy, and my whole body shook. When I took a closer look, I saw that he was Bob's brother instead. Peter had come by to pick up the flatbed trailer, which belonged to his parents. He looked just like Bob with his hat on. The way he stood, the way he moved—I thought that I was seeing a ghost! Peter was civil, but he didn't stay to socialize.

As a family, we decided that Grandma should have Bob's ashes. Braden agreed to take them down and give them to her. I don't know what she did with the ashes.

It's had always been difficult for me to go to the courthouse, because the jail is connected to it. There is a one-way street around the courthouse and jail. Male inmates stand at the narrow windows, hoping to catch a glimpse of life outside the prison walls. It makes me sad to think that this was Bob's reality at one time. I cried the whole way home every time I had to go there. This horrible place was where he spent the last months of his life, because of me. And the guilt consumed me once again.

TWELVE

Betrayal

When my father and mother forsake me, then the Lord will take care of me.

—Psalm 27:10

I thought that we had been through enough, but I was about to find out quite differently.

My dad had suffered from bone cancer for the past few years. It started out as prostate cancer. He refused medical care, and so the cancer spread. His leg became terribly swollen, and he was put on morphine. It was hard to hear the voice of this tough, rugged man who I had worshiped my whole life, say how much pain he was in.

We talked every now and then on the phone and would send each other little trinkets and letters. In June of 2001, I received a call at work from my father's stepson, Joe. I sadly asked, "Daddy's dead, isn't he?"

"Yes, he died this morning in a car accident," he said.

"A car accident?" I asked bewildered.

"Your dad was driving just down the street from his house. He somehow didn't make the corner and rolled the car."

I sat at work and wept. Fond memories flooded my mind of times spent with my dad. *I'll never see you again, Daddy.*

The funeral was to be held at the Masonic Hall in Tucson, Arizona. The boys and I left the following day. I wanted to stop by my dad's house the night before the funeral and pick up some things.

We drove twenty-three hours straight to get to Tucson. I drove until I was so exhausted that I couldn't see the road anymore, and then Braden took over and did the same. Neither of us seemed to be able to sleep when the other was driving. My mind was racing the whole trip. *Daddy owned so much stuff. What on earth are we going to do with it all? It will take a month to go through everything. How am I going to do that, living in Nebraska?* I was utterly exhausted. Toward the end of the trip, we were switching drivers every hour. My eyelids were like heavy weights that could no longer be lifted. I was viewing the dark road through tiny slits. I was amazed that we got to Tucson all in one piece.

We arrived early enough to go directly out to my dad's acreage. I wanted to see firsthand what we were dealing with. I also wanted to spend time among his things to reminisce and feel close to him. We hadn't been able to spend much time together these past few years.

His four stepsons were already there with their families. They each had a pickup, which they were loading with furniture and other items.

When I asked them, "What's going on here?" one of Daddy's stepsons, Derrick, replied, "We are just picking up our mother's things." She had passed away three years prior, but I replied, "Okay, that's fine."

I then tried to enter the house, but Derrick quickly blocked the doorway. "Why are you keeping me from my own dad's house?" I asked.

Derrick replied, "Your dad wouldn't want you to see inside the house due to the mess."

I tried to push my way around him. "I don't care about the mess, and Daddy's not around to care, either. Please step aside and let me in." Derrick was not going to budge from that doorway.

"Derrick, let me in!" I was getting pretty angry by now. I had sent my dad a lot of antiques and other items, and if nothing else, I definitely wanted those things back.

"I'm sorry, I can't do that," he said.

I finally told Braden and Jamen, "Come on. Let's get out of here." I wasn't actually planning on leaving, but I wanted Dad's stepsons to think that we were.

Braden tried sneaking up to the house to grab some things, but there were so many people milling around that he was spotted.

We waited along the roadside for night fall, far enough down the street, so as to not be seen. "As full as their trucks were, they should be leaving soon," I told Braden.

One of the stepsons spotted us while leaving the house, so we decided to leave. "We will just come back tomorrow after the funeral," I fumed.

The day of the funeral, it was a scorching 104-degree day. My sister, Wendy, was in town with her husband, Tom. We met for lunch and decided to go up to Sabino Canyon to keep cool until the funeral.

We arrived just in time to catch the last trolley going up into the canyon. The air was cool and refreshing. There were ponds in the mountains from the snow melt. We got off the trolley to soak our feet in the tepid water and enjoy the scenery. I hadn't seen Wendy since Mama's funeral, so it was great to spend sisterly time together.

"We tried to go out to Daddy's house last night, and those four boys wouldn't let us through the door," I told her.

She admitted, "We went out there, too, and were turned away. I don't know what's going on, but they were sure loading up their trucks quickly. Something really stinks here, and I don't like it one bit. But for now we need to head back to Tucson and get ready for the funeral. Let's meet up afterward and go back out there."

Tom and Wendy arrived at the funeral before we did. She was met in the parking lot by one of the stepsons and promptly handed a copy of my dad's will. She studied it and came to an abrupt stop when she read my father's words, "I intentionally leave nothing to my two natural daughters, Wendy and Lori." His signature was hand written next to it to authenticate that this was indeed his wishes.

When we arrived, she handed the will to me and said, "Sister, you've got to read this."

When I read those words, my heart came to a complete stop. "I can't believe this! Why is he doing this to us?" I asked.

Wendy shrugged her shoulders, "I don't know, Sister."

From all the pain that I had experienced in the past, nothing could compare to the pain that I felt at that moment. My dad had hurt me so much more than Bob ever could have, with just that one sentence. Bruises heal, but when someone hurts your heart, it is a much deeper wound.

"I just want to leave here now and go back home!" I exclaimed.

Wendy took me by the arm, "No. We came here to say goodbye to Daddy. We are going to march right in there and not let those boys defeat us." Together, we grudgingly went in.

The front rows were all seated when we arrived. Wendy and I had to sit toward the back of the room, like we were not even part of the family. My dad's sister, Grace, and her daughter, Liz, sat with us. They were both stunned when I showed them a copy of the will. "I'm so sorry. I can't believe he would do that to his own daughters," they said.

"If I didn't see his signature, I wouldn't have believed it myself," I replied.

We all sat numbly through the strangest funeral that I have ever been to in my life. It was a Masonic funeral, with rituals that were reserved for the eyes of Masons only. My dad had been a Shriner clown known as "Salty."

I remember four men who were dressed in strange attire, each carrying something symbolic to the front of the lodge. One item was a white lambskin apron. In Masonic symbolism, the Lambskin Apron holds precedence. It is the initial gift of Freemasonry to a candidate, and at the end of his life, it is reverently placed on his mortal remains and buried with his body in the grave. Another item was the Sprig of Acacia. This symbolizes immortality. Wendy and I looked at each other with questioning looks. *Where is God in all of this?*

There was a time for people to reflect and say nice things about my dad. Liz was furious by this point at the way we were being treated. She brazenly announced, "I would just like for you to meet Earl's real children," and she had me and Wendy stand up. She wanted everyone to know that we were his children, not the four stepsons taking up the entire front row with their families. The four brothers smiled to each other, seemingly to truly enjoy all of this.

I leaned over to Wendy and said, "I can't believe he chose them over his own daughters. If he had any issues with us, he should have at least left something to his grandkids." All she could do was shake her head.

I thought that my dad would have a military funeral, since he had served in the Navy and Air Force. He retired from the Seabees, a construction battalion. I would have chosen a dignified military funeral for a man who had served his country so faithfully. The stepsons had seen to all of the arrangements, however. It was almost like we had never existed.

I was angry and hurt. I had spent my life placing my dad so high on a pedestal that I thought could never be brought down. I was proud of him, and in a single moment, all of that admiration was stripped away.

At the end of the service, Wendy turned to me and said, "I guess we are never going to hear those three little words that I have waited my whole life to hear: I love you."

I quietly replied, "No, it doesn't appear so."

His step-children were to be his sole heirs. After the funeral, one of the boys approached me and my sister and said, "You may each choose something that is leftover from one of the display tables."

"How gracious of you to allow us to take a little trinket home from our own father's funeral," I sarcastically replied. At this point, I was so angry that I didn't want to take anything. I knew that I would come to regret it later, though. My sister wanted his badge. I grudgingly took his sheriff's hat and a shooting trophy. Jamen chose his clown shoes. Braden refrained from taking anything.

As Wendy was inspecting her fortune, she found a $100 bill hidden behind the badge and promptly gave me half. "I'm so surprised that those boys didn't find the money and keep that, too," she said.

We had been promised so many things from my dad. He had called recently to say, "I'm going to send Braden a rifle and several holsters that I want him to have." Instead, he had gone to the hospital for treatment and never sent the package.

We sat with family and friends at the luncheon after the funeral. Everyone was in shock with the news that we had been disowned.

Grace said, "Your dad loved both of you girls. Really, he did."

"I can't really feel the love right now," I flatly replied, pushing the food around my plate. "If Daddy loved us, he wouldn't have done this to us."

A long time coworker of my dad approached me and said, "I'm so sorry for your loss. Your dad was one of the finest men I know." One of the stepsons, Bill, was standing directly behind the man and looked at me. I looked past the man offering the condolences, glared directly at Bill, and vehemently said, "My dad may have been a great man, but in the end, he disowned me and my sister. So, I'm not really very happy with him at this particular moment." The bewildered man walked off, and Bill smugly smiled back. How I wanted to reach out and smack him!

There was no internment. He chose to be cremated and wanted his ashes spread in the ocean. I never saw the urn. My dad's best friends, Hoss and Angie, invited us over to their home after the funeral. We accepted their offer. I needed some time to make sense out of all this.

We drove to the country to spend the afternoon with them. They were equally bewildered at my dad's betrayal. We were about to leave when Hoss said, "Just a minute, I have something for Braden," and handed him a leather working kit and a holster that Daddy had made. "Here, I think your grandpa would want you to have these. He left them here, but you should have them."

Braden responded, "Thank you. This means a lot to me to have something that was special to him."

For a brief moment, I was able to forget my pain.

The boys and I got a hotel room in Tucson that night. My sister called me, "We have been looking all evening for a room but can't find anything reasonable."

I told her, "Our room has an extra bed. Why don't you come and bunk with us?"

This gave us extra time to commiserate together. Wendy was handling everything much better than I was. She told me, "You know, I would expect this for myself, since Daddy and I were not that close, but to disown you, that shocks me."

I was feeling especially low and told Wendy, "I am not deserving of anyone's love, nor am I am capable of loving." Bob had made me feel so worthless.

She grabbed hold of my hands and assured me, "You have a lot of love to give, and you are a very special person. God has someone special out there that will love you deeply."

I felt so betrayed. I yelled, "Daddy, you knew we lost everything in the fire; I really could have used your help right about now! I can't believe that you chose those boys over your own daughters! How could you do this to us?" I held onto my pain for over a year. I wanted to punish him by refusing to forgive him.

I heard later from my aunt that my dad was contemplating changing his will to include me and my sister, and I learned something about procrastination. Never put things off until tomorrow; you don't know if tomorrow will come. Daddy felt that he had time before the illness killed him.

He had listed me and Wendy as beneficiaries on his retirement policies, but had also chosen to have the benefits cease upon death. In choosing that option, he got more retirement money while he was alive. *Why even bother to put us on as beneficiaries when the State of Arizona would receive the remainder of the retirement money?*

My sister and I each received $100. I felt it was another slap in the face by my dad.

Wendy suggested, "Let's do something frivolous with the $100, something to remember Daddy by! I think we should each buy a ring."

"I don't really feel like remembering Daddy right now," I replied.

"Oh, come on. Let's have some fun with this."

"Fine, I will go buy a ring," I forced myself to say.

I chose a simple ring with an emerald stone, set in yellow gold. It was a painful reminder, however, and I put the ring away.

We didn't contest the will, although I thought we should have. By all rights, we were entitled to at least half of all that he owned. Our reasoning was that we were both too far away to hire lawyers to fight it and that the legal fees would eat up anything that we would have been awarded. Wendy's viewpoint was, "Daddy didn't want us to have anything, so I don't feel that we should pursue it." The pain was too fresh for me to think rationally.

"Sister, you're looking at this all wrong," Wendy said. "Those boys will have all that money used up in no time. Our rewards are eternal in heaven, and none of this is going to matter at all."

I muttered something under my breath, and we said our goodbyes.

The drive home seemed to take forever. I felt like we had just wasted three days, and a lot of money that we didn't have, by traveling to a funeral of someone who had discarded us.

When we pulled up into the yard, we were met with a lake in our front lawn. "What now?" I screamed.

We discovered that a pipe had burst in the well house while we were gone. Who knows how long the water had been running nonstop? *I wonder how much my electric bill is going to be for this?* Braden went into town and purchased the supplies to repair the damage. He was able to fix the pipe for $1.85. What an encouragement and blessing he was to have around at such a difficult time.

Three years had passed since my dad's death when our pastor preached about forgiveness. He said, "It will eat you up inside and make you bitter if you don't let it go. You are not hurting anyone but yourself." He went on, "It will also cause a broken fellowship with God. The Bible says that He will not hear the prayers of one who cannot forgive." I felt like he was speaking directly to me. I definitely needed God, and needed Him to hear my prayers.

Afterward, I asked our Pastor, "How do you forgive someone who is dead?"

He explained, "You set up a chair and put their picture on it. Yell, scream, and cry, letting them know how badly they have hurt you. Then you tell them, 'I forgive you, the slate has been wiped clean, and it won't be held against you anymore.' You document all of this on a piece of paper and put it in your Bible or another safe place. Whenever Satan wants to bring it up to you, again, you can say, 'No! I forgave him on this date, the slate has been wiped clean, and he has been forgiven.'"

Easier said than done.

Later that evening, I was finally ready to follow his instructions. I wanted to be freed from this anger that was consuming me. I set a picture of Daddy in the chair, yelled and screamed at him: "You really hurt me, Daddy! Why did you do this to me? What did I ever do to deserve this? I have spent my whole life trying to please you, and you betrayed me!"

My ranting continued until I was totally spent. Then I was finally able to say, "I forgive you, Daddy. I don't understand, but I forgive you." As I spoke those last words, the bitterness and anger left me like a huge weight had been lifted off of my shoulders. *I'm free! I'm finally free!*

At times, I do wonder why he chose to disown us. Maybe God knew how difficult it could be with step-brothers and wanted to spare us all the trouble. I would like to ask my dad about that someday. Hopefully, I will see him again to ask him. I wish I knew if he had made it to heaven.

Wendy shared a story with me of why she believes that he is in heaven. She said, "When I was about nine years old, Daddy told me about heaven, and hell, and about the salvation that Jesus offers. So I really believe that he is saved." It gave me a glimmer of hope to hold onto, that I would see him again one day.

I know in my heart that I have truly forgiven my dad, because I can talk about the situation but no longer feel the hurt and pain that was consuming me.

Sometimes, I felt like we had suffered more than our fair share, while so many others seem to go through life unscathed. There were so many tragedies so close together that it was almost overwhelming. God promised that he would not give us more than we could bear (1 Corinthians 10:13), and I feel like I should be the strongest person in the world by now. He gave us just enough strength to get through that day, and then the next day, and the next.

You would never know the pain we have been through by looking at us, just like we don't know the pain that someone else has been through. Often times, we don't see the pain behind the smile. Proverbs 14:13 says, "Even in laughter, the heart may ache." I try to keep this in mind when dealing with a difficult person.

THIRTEEN

Answered Prayer

*It shall come to pass, that before they call, I will answer; and
while they are still speaking, I will hear.*
—Isaiah 65:24

When Braden was fourteen, he had ridden his dirt bike on a trail way out
in the middle of nowhere. When he returned home a few hours later, I
noticed that he was not wearing the watch that had become a permanent
fixture on his wrist.

"Where's your watch, Braden?" I asked.

"Well . . . I was riding my bike when I hit a huge bump. I went flying
in one direction, and my bike went flying in another. Then I noticed that
my watch was gone."

"Your dad will be furious. We need to find that watch!" I said with
urgency.

"Mom, I looked everywhere for it, for the past two hours. That's why
I was gone for so long. It's just not there!"

I told him, "I will go out with you and help you look."

He shook his head in discouragement, "It's not going to do any
good."

"Well, we have to try. Go get in the car."

When we arrived at the location of where he said that the bike had
hit, I stopped the car and prayed, "Lord Jesus, you know exactly where
his watch is. Please reveal it so that I can show him how real You are." I
opened my eyes and walked a few feet over to a tree. I reached up and
took his watch out of the branch where it had landed. I then turned and
handed it to him.

He looked at me with amazement and said, "How did you do that?"

I told him, "God knew exactly where your watch was, and He cares about everything that you care about." *I sure wish that all of our prayers could be answered so quickly!*

When Braden was fifteen, he worked the summer as a lifeguard. He had saved up all of his money to buy a transmission for a used Porsche 924 that he was fixing up. A transmission came up on eBay. Braden had placed a bid on the transmission but lost the bid. A seller contacted Braden and said, "I saw that you lost the bid on the Porsche transmission, but I happen to have one for sale for $525.00." The man gave Braden all of his information to put him at ease. Braden sent the cashier's check as requested and waited for the transmission to arrive.

I contacted the seller several times in the following two weeks. "I had trouble finding a big enough box. Don't worry. I will send it out very soon," he replied. So, again we waited.

Two months went by, with no word from the seller. I called and left a message on his answering machine explaining to him, "My son worked hard all summer to earn that money. Now, do the right thing and send him the transmission." After no reply, I contacted eBay's support group and emailed the police department in Louisiana, where this man lived, to file a complaint. I also began to pray.

God knew exactly who this man was and where he was at that precise moment. The Louisiana police department told me that complaints had to be made in person. We lived in Nebraska, so that was not an option. Every day for eight months, I prayed for God to open doors and to provide a way to get Braden's money returned. Enough time had passed that I finally gave up. I cleared the files out of my computer and decided that God's will was to let this go.

A week after I deleted the files, I received an email from the Louisiana police department. They wrote, "Office policy has recently changed. We are now able to accept complaints via email. We have spoken to the man in question recently, as there were many complaints against him. What would you like for us to do?"

I quickly replied, "All I want is my son's money back."

The police then told the seller, "You can return the money for the transmission, or go to jail. It's your choice." Two weeks later, a check came in the mail for $525. God needed me to let go, quit interfering, and let Him work. It was great to show Braden that we have an awesome God, who has no limitations and who cares about what concerns us. He has the power to open or close any door that He chooses and is able to do abundantly above all that we ask or think, no matter what the distance.

God is definitely not a genie in a bottle, subject to our whims and desires, but He does long to reveal Himself to an unbelieving world through answering prayer on our behalf.

FOURTEEN

Moving on with life

*As for God, His way is perfect; The word of the Lord is proven;
He is a shield to all who trust in Him.*

—Psalm 18:30

I have discovered that God brought people into my life to help me through difficult times. They were put there to offer wisdom, support, and to cry with me. They have prayed with me and stood by me through all of my doubting, anger, and fear. They allowed me to vent and guided me through to the wonderful things that were to come.

I was now a woman alone with two teenage sons, making decisions that I was ill-equipped to make. It became my job to maintain the pasture and repair vehicles that were continually breaking down. I wish now that I would have paid more attention to Bob when he was trying to teach me these things. He had always taken care of all of the outside things. Now it was my job, and it was overwhelming. I considered selling the pasture, but I loved it there. I loved to stand outside and drink in the beauty of it.

I have always enjoyed the view of the pasture outside the kitchen window. In the past, I had been on the lookout for Bob's white T-shirt to keep track of where he was. As I looked out after he died, I could still see glimpses of his white shirt moving, off in the distance, like he was still tending to the pasture. He loved it out there so much.

I had been trying to clean up around the place. It was a calm, sunny day, so I gathered burnable debris and burned it in a clearing surrounded by grass. When the fire was out and there was just a little trail of smoke left, Braden suggested, "Let's go to town and look for a car."

I should douse the embers before we leave, but it's pretty well died down. It should be alright.

The wind picked up while we were gone. When we were just about home, I could see thick black smoke coming from the direction of our pasture. Fear overcame me, and I prayed, "Not again! Lord, please. Don't let it be our home, again!"

We drove home at a much faster pace now. My heart sank when I saw that our pasture was engulfed in flames. The beautiful pine trees that Bob had planted for our windbreak were ablaze. Our garage was right at the south edge of the fire, with Braden's Porsche in it. Praise God, the wind was blowing in the opposite direction and the garage was spared. The fire was headed straight for the neighbor's farm across the road. "It's going to jump the road and burn Orin's hay stacks!" I screamed.

Just then, the fire department arrived. Thankfully, someone had seen the smoke and called them. The fire was contained before it was able to cross the road. We have always believed in donating to the fire department each year. You never know when you are going to need them, some of us more than others.

A few dozen of our trees were gone. The fire had consumed about ten acres of pasture. Bob would have been sickened to see the destruction; all of his hard work up in flames.

The fire chief told me, "The winds are supposed to shift tonight and will be coming straight toward the house." He stressed, "I need you to go out every so often and make sure that none of the fires start up again. Can you do that?"

I nodded yes.

He said, "I hereby dub you 'Sparky.' Now I will kindly ask you to abstain from setting any more fires."

"I think you're right," I replied, while giving him a scout's honor sign.

I heeded his advice and went out every hour throughout the night, carrying buckets of water and a hoe. Each time I went out, I found several new fires that had started in the dead debris under the trees.

During the next two years after his dad's death, Jamen sought the solace of friends, spending most of his spare time with them. I didn't complain. He needed them to help him through all that had happened. They all had four-wheelers and spent many hours riding together. He asked, "Mom, I'd really like to ride with my friends. Can we use part of my social security money to buy a four-wheeler?"

After some consideration, I agreed. I didn't want him to feel left out, but I also reasoned, "Maybe this will help him to forget things for a little while and just have some fun."

Jamen struggled through school. He was a popular boy in high school, but studies were not a top priority for him. I didn't force the issue. It was hard enough to be a teenager without all that he had been through. I was thankful that my kids had good friends. They played such an important part in the healing process.

Braden preferred quiet nights at home doing homework, and he enjoyed the luxury of watching TV whenever he wanted. He and his friends went bowling every Wednesday night.

He graduated from high school in 2002, doing very well his senior year. He then went on to the local college and majored in biology. He was on the president's list for his grades, even while holding down a full-time job working at the airport. His dad had said, "Braden will never go to college because he lacks the skills necessary to study." I think Bob would be really proud of what Braden has accomplished.

I feel blessed that I had good boys. I don't know how I would have made it through otherwise.

FIFTEEN

Life sure seems unfair

We are hard-pressed on every side, yet not crushed; we are perplexed, but not in despair; persecuted, but not forsaken; struck down, but not destroyed.
—2 Corinthians 4: 8-9

Two years after my dad's death, I received an email from a law firm stating, "Earl Worthington obtained a $100,000 life insurance policy a month prior to his death. Wendy Russell is listed as the sole beneficiary on the policy. We are trying to locate Ms. Russell. If you happen to have her home address, we will get the necessary paperwork to her." I quickly replied, giving them her information.

"Yes! Things are finally starting to look up for us!" I screamed. I excitedly emailed Wendy to let her know what was going on. As soon as she received the paperwork, she supplied the information requested and waited with great anticipation.

Two months dragged by. She finally got a discouraging letter from the insurance company. They offered several excuses why they didn't want to pay the claim. First, my dad had just obtained the policy. They said the policy hadn't gone into effect yet because he hadn't paid the first premium. The other excuse was that he was under the influence of alcohol when he crashed, but they had no evidence to substantiate that claim. *Under the influence of morphine was a better possibility.*

Finally, after a year of dealing with the insurance company, they agreed to pay Wendy a pittance of $1000.

Without any reservation, she sent me $500. I took my newfound wealth and bought a new refrigerator. I said a little "thank you" to Daddy every time that I opened the refrigerator door.

A month later, we learned that my dad had also obtained another $100,000 insurance policy. Derrick, one of the stepsons, was the sole beneficiary on that one. Miraculously, that policy was paid out to him. *If one policy was denied, wouldn't the other one be also?*

I was furious! I didn't want to be greedy, but Wendy and I sure could have used some help right about now. Once again, I had to remind Satan, "I have forgiven my dad." But I questioned, "Why does this keep happening to us?" Life sure seemed to be unfair!

Three years after the fire, I was digging through the debris pile, still searching for that elusive ring from my mother. I stopped dead in my tracks when I saw remnants of $100 bills lying in the rubble. I screamed at Bob, "Why a stupid flammable shoebox! Why didn't you put the money somewhere where it would have been safe?"

Then I focused my anger on God, "We were in the house for a week. Why couldn't we have found that shoebox in that time? What would it have hurt? I just want to know why!" I wailed.

I didn't get a reply from either of them.

I gathered as much of the money that I could find and sent the fragments to the Federal Reserve Bank to see if they could determine enough to reimburse me. Early in 2006, the Federal Reserve sent me a letter that they could not determine what any of the money was, due to the destroyed serial numbers. I broke down and cried. I regretted working all those years, saving all that money, and putting my boys in daycare for nothing but a pile of ashes. Someday, I hoped that God will show me why all of this had to take place.

One day, I cried out to God, "Lord, I can't handle all of this. It's just too much for me to bear! I'm giving You all of my pain and hurt, because I can't deal with it anymore." The burden was lifted, and I felt at peace for the first time in quite a while.

I had forgiven my dad, but I didn't really feel like I needed to forgive Bob. I felt more sympathy towards him than anger, knowing that he wasn't really mean, but in need of treatment.

I thought I had healed, but a search on an unclaimed property website in 2011 sliced open an old wound. I typed in my maiden name and waited for the list of property owners to appear. I stared in shock as the name of my father, Earl Mason Worthington, materialized. The property was located in New Mexico. *What property would you have in New Mexico?*

"Can you claim this property?" the screen asked. I broke down and cried. "No, I can't! I'm not his heir." Bitterness consumed me. Do I tell his stepsons, and rightful heirs, about more of my dad's money that is owed them? Or do I remain silent? Why would I want them to have one more cent of my dad's money?

I contacted the New Mexico State Treasurer to attempt filing a claim. They required documentation that I could not produce. I sought wise counsel from friends that I didn't really want to hear: "What would God have you do? He could use this in a mighty way."

"I don't want to ask Him. The pain is too deep right now." But I couldn't escape what was the right thing to do. I located the address of one of the stepsons. "My sister and I are still very hurt over this," I wrote. "But I asked God what He wanted me to do. I am not the heir and cannot file a claim, and so I have enclosed the necessary papers and information that you will need." I set the envelope on my desk. *Maybe I should think about this for awhile.*

A picture of my dad dressed as 'Salty the Clown' lay on a chair in the storage room. He was wearing a pouty whimpering look that seemed to mock me. The pain of his betrayal surfaced again. I couldn't bear to look at him, and turned the photograph over.

A few days later I was ready to mail the letter. I slipped the envelope into the mail slot, hanging on to the corner of it. *Lord, I pray for your blessing over this.* I released the letter, and at the same time was able to let go of the situation. *I forgive you Daddy, and I might have to forgive you again tomorrow.*

SIXTEEN

Mr. Right

Love bears all things, believes all things, hopes all things, endures
all things. Love never fails. And now abide faith, hope, love,
these three; but the greatest of these is love.

—I Corinthians 13

I worked full time at the insurance agency while keeping the house and pasture running as best I could. We were in church every week and trying to heal. I couldn't seem to escape the guilt that was consuming me. Every night, my pillow was soaked from crying myself to sleep.

I had been alone for two and a half years since we were taken to the shelter. I didn't think that I would ever want to be close to a man again, and yet the loneliness overtook me. *I shouldn't even be contemplating ruining someone else's life, the way that I ruined Bob's.*

I prayed about my situation, and one day, I decided to make a list. It was an extensive list of the qualities that I would like in a man. I left nothing out, even down to the sound of his voice. I wanted someone who was especially gentle, easy going, and not named Bob. The chance of finding this perfect man was remote, to say the least. Still, I prayed on this list every day and gave God my pain. *Is there someone out there who would truly love me?*

Instead of leaving it for God to handle, I went off on my own and registered on an Internet dating service.

A man from Omaha saw my profile. "Would you like to go bowling and out to dinner?" he asked.

"Sure, that sounds great," I replied.

"Could you wear a short skirt to go bowling in?" he said, and then laughed.

"I'll see you at 7:00, and I'll be wearing jeans," I firmly replied.

I was extremely nervous since I hadn't dated in a very long time. He was late, and I was pacing the hall when the phone rang. "You won't believe this, but I was halfway to your place when the transmission blew up in my truck."

I was disappointed, but replied, "That's okay. Some other time then."

Later, I thanked God for intervening. I secretly thought that God had blown up his transmission to protect me. He was not the man for me, and we never met. Had I been busy getting to know this man, I might have missed the man that God had intended for me.

Why do I settle for second best when God has the very best pre-selected for me?

Again I went back to my list and prayed, this time trying to leave it to God. One time when I was praying, I distinctly heard a still small voice say, "He's not ready yet."

Of all the men in the world, how will I know who this one man is?

In April of 2002, my friend Kally was going to a fireman's dance. Her husband, Rob, would be busy taking tickets. "Lori, you have to come to the dance with me tonight!" she pleaded.

"I don't really feel like going to a dance," I replied.

"Come on. Rob will be busy and I don't want to sit there alone. Please, please come with me!" she implored.

"Oh, fine. For you, I'll go," I said reluctantly.

At 9:00 P.M., I was just about to call her to cancel. It was time to start getting ready for bed, not to be going out. Kally wasn't feeling well and was about to call me to cancel, also, but in the end, neither of us cancelled and we both ended up at the dance.

An acquaintance at our table asked me to dance a few times. Bob had never taken me dancing in the past twenty years, and I self-consciously stumbled my way through a few turns around the floor.

On the other side of the darkly lit room sat several men, along with Arlene, one of my coworkers. One of the men asked her, "Are there any single girls here for my friend to dance with?" Arlene looked around the room and pointed out a young woman.

"No, she's not my type. I want someone closer to my own age."

Arlene scanned the room again and pointed to me. "She's single. Why don't you go ask her to dance?"

He balked until his friend said, "I'm going to go over there and ask her for you if you don't."

"I can ask a girl to dance myself!" he replied.

The man sauntered over and asked me, "Would you care to dance?"

I looked up at him and said, "You want to dance with me? I'm really not a very good dancer." With pleading eyes, I looked over to Kally for help.

She pushed me toward the stranger and said, "Go dance and have fun."

"Maybe just one dance," I said. I stood up and whispered back at Kally, "You're going to get it when I come back." She was busy giggling. I turned and looked this man in the face for the first time. He was nice looking, with graying hair and blue-grey eyes. His smile was warm, which cast away some of my fear.

"My name is Glenn," he said, as he gently reached out, took me in his arms, and danced the two-step with me.

"I'm Lori," I yelled over the music.

He abruptly stopped. "My ex-wife's name was Lori."

Despite that, he asked me to dance again. I was embarrassed, because I continually stepped on his feet. After every dance, we went back to our own tables. It gave us time to talk to our friends about each other. Kally was eager to hear all the details. "Who is he? Where's he from? Do you like him?"

For nearly every dance, he was standing there with his hand out for me to take and dance with him. One time, though, he was busy talking with his friend. The man at our table quickly asked me to dance. I was headed out to the dance floor with him when Glenn started over. I flashed him the "you snooze, you lose" look. He lifted up his hands in surrender and went back to his chair. I noticed that he kept watching me, however. He was a bit more "Johnny on the spot" for the remainder of the dances that night. Kally decided to leave at around 11:00 P.M. As I watched her leave, I had a twinge of remorse that I hadn't been very good company for her.

Glenn came over and asked, "Why don't you come and sit with me?" I felt very comfortable with him, so I sat down at his table. We had so much to talk about: It was like we were old friends. When the dance was over, he walked me to my car and we talked more.

It was going on 3:00 A.M. when Glenn said, "I have to get up in a few hours, so I need to get home. Can I call you sometime?"

"I would really like that, but I don't know that I should start dating at this time. I have my two boys at home, and they have been through a lot of change already. The timing just isn't quite right. But I had a really great time tonight. If I change my mind, I will get a hold of you."

"I understand," he said. "Goodnight."

He walked down the street to where his car was parked. I waved as he drove past in his cherry red Monte Carlo. With a huge smile, he waved back. I felt like a giddy school girl the rest of the night.

Two weeks passed and I couldn't get him out of my mind. He had so many qualities that I liked in a man. I didn't feel afraid of him at all, so I decided to call him.

A week went by with no response from him, and I was beginning to feel that maybe he wasn't the one after all. Then one night, he called, "Would you like to go out for pizza?"

"Sure, I'll meet you there," I replied, just in case he was a homicidal maniac.

I arrived a few minutes early, got a table, and anxiously waited until he arrived. "Sorry I was late. I was talking to my mom on the phone," Glenn said. So far, I was impressed.

We spent the evening talking nervously. Neither of us had dated in a long time, and everything was rather awkward. It shouldn't have been this difficult since we had talked for hours at the dance just weeks before and we had been relatively at ease with each other.

As we talked, we found that we had so much in common. We had both lived in Arizona, worked on center pivot irrigation systems, and were both Baptist. I could listen to his tranquil voice all night. He was handsome and intelligent, but what I was most attracted to was his gentleness. We then had that awkward moment of saying goodnight, finally parting with a handshake. I replayed the night in my head on the drive home and wondered if he was thinking about me, too.

My heart sank when Glenn called a few days later and admitted that he was a bit hesitant about starting a relationship with me. "So much has happened to you. I'm afraid that you might have too much baggage," he said.

So, he doesn't want a basket case! I was a little miffed by his implication.

"It's true that I had a lot of baggage. But I couldn't deal with it, and I had to give it to God. I couldn't carry around the heavy burden any more. I am not bitter or holding grudges. I have been able to forgive Bob and my dad," I replied.

A week later, Glenn decided to take a chance on me and called to ask me out again. He came over and helped me with some projects, and met the boys. We spent the evening talking. As I got to know him better, I started checking things off of my list that I had been praying on. He met most of the qualities that I had asked for.

One day, he rode up on his red 1976 BMW motorcycle. He got off, opened up his saddlebag, and handed me a semi-wilted purple flower that he had picked for me. *He was thinking about me on the way up here!* My heart melted. It was the nicest gift that I had received in a long time. I pressed it in my Bible, to hold onto that day.

He came over every Saturday to spend the day with me and help out with the continued cleanup. He was always a gentleman and never tried to kiss me.

After a month, I was growing more concerned. *I hope he's not gay.* I know he was married once, but sometimes marriage is a cover-up. I really liked him and hoped that wasn't the case. *There's only one way to find out.* Before he left that night, I grabbed on to his lapels, pulled him close to me, and kissed him. He didn't kiss me back, but just stood there looking at me. So I kissed him again, and still no response. I would have received more of a response from kissing the back of my hand! Bewildered, I said, "Goodnight," then turned and went back to the house. *Yep! He's definitely gay! Darn! He was such a great guy, too.*

Glenn showed up again the following night. "I wanted to talk to you about what happened last night. I needed to look you in the eye to see what you were expecting out of this relationship," he calmly stated.

I thought it was clear. "Generally, you date someone to get to know them, and if you fall in love with that person, then marriage would be the next step," I honestly replied.

"When you kiss someone, you have moved beyond friendship. I don't know if I want any emotional involvement at this point in time. I really just wanted a friend——a girl to have fun with, where there are no strings attached," he confessed.

My pride was a bit wounded, but I managed to reply, "I guess I misunderstood and thought that you wanted the same thing I did."

"I want a buddy, not a girlfriend. I really do want to kiss you but only if it doesn't become personal," he replied.

Doesn't become personal? What does that mean? "Honestly I was beginning to think you were gay," I timidly said.

"No, I'm not gay!" he said with a hint of aggravation.

We both stood looking each other in the eye, daring the other to make a move. *He's going to cave. He already admitted that he wanted to kiss me. It's just a matter of time now.*

Then, he changed his mind and decided to kiss me, probably wanting to prove that he wasn't gay. Much to my relief, he kissed very well. From then on, he was not so reluctant to kiss me goodnight. *So much for just being friends!*

We continued to see each other once a week. I would have preferred more attention, but he did help keep my mind off of Bob, and the grief and guilt that I had been feeling.

Glenn had been alone for more than eight years when we met, and I was the first girl that he had dated since his divorce. He loved his freedom and enjoyed coming and going as he pleased. He was reluctant to have his lifestyle change.

We had a great time whenever we were together. It was nice to have fun again; it had been so long. He was so gentle with me. I felt safe and girlishly happy. I didn't believe that I would ever feel this way again.

One of my dreams was to live in a real house, not a trailer. I had lived in a trailer for half of my life, and I longed for sturdy floors, walls that didn't buckle in the wind, and pipes that didn't freeze every winter. Glenn lived in a two-story brick farmhouse built around 1910. We had been dating for two months when he told me, "You can come live with me someday, and I could be your husband." He immediately wondered why he had blurted that out. I was encouraged by his comment, though.

Six months after we started dating, I asked him to come to my church. He agreed to come the next week but was unimpressed. I told him, "Well, if your church is so much better, then you can bring me to your church."

It took quite a bit of prodding before he gave in and took me. "A man just doesn't take a girl to church unless they are serious, in my opinion," he confessed. Even though he was quite reluctant, he did take me the following week.

After the service, I said to him, "You're right, I can see why you love your church. The pastor was great, and the people are warm and friendly."

I felt comfortable right away and made several new friends. After asking me about my faith, the pastor gave me the thumbs-up sign, which set Glenn's mind more at ease.

Glenn decided, "Since church was so easy, maybe I'll take you to meet my family."

"I'm sad that you never had the chance to meet either of my parents. I think they would have liked you very much," I said.

His family was holding a reunion at the senior center in Madison. I nervously entered the building and was shocked at the number of people there were in his immediate family. All ten brothers and sisters lived in close proximity to each other, and each year, they got together. I had never been to a family reunion before.

Thinking back to Bob and how he treated his family, I told Glenn, "I am going to be watching you very closely for any warning flags." Family contention was such a foreign notion to him that he didn't know what I meant.

Glenn immediately disappeared to the other side of the room with the guys, while I was left standing alone! I stood there looking dumbfounded. *You just lost a lot of points with me, Buster.*

His five sisters were thrilled to see that he brought someone along. One by one, they came over to sit with me and they asked so many questions. His sister, Millie, told him, "Don't worry, Glenn. We'll check her out for you." This time, I watched closely how he interacted with his family. I wasn't going to get caught in that trap again.

I was quite pleased to see that everyone genuinely loved and respected each other. I overheard conversations of how they could help each other out. I liked this family; it reminded me of my relationship with my mom and it felt very comfortable. They accepted me as one of their own from the very beginning.

For the next six hours, his sisters talked with me and introduced me to the rest of the family. I was enjoying myself, but I didn't appreciate being ignored by Glenn.

On the way home, I said as gently as I could, "So you took me to meet your family, but I wasn't introduced to a soul. Then you disappeared to the other side of the room for the remainder of the day leaving me to fend for myself."

He grinned and said, "I was keeping an eye on you from across the room and saw that my sisters were doing a good job of keeping you company."

"I went there to be with you, not to be watched from afar for six hours," I replied with a twinge of disgust. He did not get his points back.

We had been dating for eight months as Christmas was approaching. Glenn confided to me, "I really don't know what to get you for Christmas."

Shyly I said, "I would like a ring, something that says that I am taken." He pondered that for a while, secretly wishing that I wanted anything but that.

Christmas arrived and he handed me a small white box. I excitedly opened it and found a delicate Black Hills gold ring with a diamond chip in the center. I cried, "Oh, a promise ring! Just what I wanted."

He firmly stated, "It is not a promise ring."

I teased, "You obviously don't know what a promise ring is, because this is in fact a promise ring."

This was a great source of contention with him. Regardless, I was happy to have his ring on my finger to show the world that I belonged to him.

I couldn't take my eyes off of my beautiful ring and dreamed of the day when I would belong to Glenn forever.

In April, we celebrated one year of dating. I liked so many qualities in this wonderful man. In looking at my list, he met everything but one. He was in debt. I was not in debt and didn't want to acquire someone else's debt should we marry. But I knew in my heart that this was the man that God had been preparing for me.

Glenn loved being with me but definitely did not want a commitment. He had been hurt before and didn't want to go through that again. There seemed to be an impenetrable fortress built around him, and yet, I sensed that he longed to be close to someone. He told me several times, "I love you, but I'm not 'in love' with you." He still considered our relationship to be more of a buddy thing, but he would speak of our future often, like he was honestly thinking about it. Most of the time, I went home thoroughly confused because of all the mixed signals.

One day, I was shopping at the Goodwill thrift store, looking at dresses. On the end of the rack was a beautiful wedding dress. It was just what I would have wanted if I were getting married. The clerks urged me,

"Go ahead and try it on." I was in no hurry, so I did. When I slipped it on, it was a perfect fit. It was a gorgeous, southern belle dress, the kind that requires wearing a hoop skirt underneath. The top came just off of my shoulders, and the bottom was pulled into scallops held up by rosettes. I felt like I could be in the movie, *Gone With the Wind*, and the best part was, it was only $25. I knew if I passed it up, one so perfect would not become available again, so I bought it. I hid it away in my closet, knowing that someday he would ask me to marry him.

SEVENTEEN

Mr. Wrong?

*Wait on the Lord; Be of good courage, and He shall strengthen
your heart; Wait, I say on the Lord!*
—Psalms 27:14

A year and a half into our relationship, Glenn called me. "I'm sorry, but
this just isn't going to work out. I love being with you, but I do not want
to get married again. Plus, you 'mother' me, and I don't need another
mother."

"Because it was late last night and I suggested that you go home, since
you were exhausted? That's why you are breaking up with me?" I huffed.

"I don't want to be told what to do," he replied.

I was absolutely devastated. I thought that God had brought him into
my life. I was now extremely confused, thinking that I had misread God's
signals. I tried to give back my ring, but Glenn told me, "It was a gift to
you. Keep it."

Then I considered the wedding dress hidden in my closet. *Great, now
what am I going to do with that?*

Our friends at church were upset about the break-up. They also
thought that we were a match made in heaven. We all began to pray about
the situation. At first my prayers were selfish. *Lord, Please bring him back
to me! I love him and don't want to lose him.* He was everything I had prayed
for and had wanted in a mate, and so I chased him. I called him from time
to time to tell him something important. I continued to go to his church,
and I would make sure to shake his hand and say hello. I wore a pretty
dress and carefully groomed myself each Sunday morning. I just happened
to sit in his line of vision since he sat in the same seat each week. *If he*

doesn't see me, he will forget about me. It was very awkward, and I was being a regular nuisance.

After two months of torturing myself, I decided that I had to pray for God's will in this and not mine. *Lord, my methods don't appear to be working too well. I don't want to repeat what I've been through in the past. If you remove him from my life, it has to be for a reason. Maybe you have something even better for me. I am letting go of this situation and allowing you to deal with it.* I was defeated, and there was nothing I could do but turn it completely over to God.

I called and left a final message on Glenn's machine. "I won't be bothering you again and will leave you alone from now on. I'm so sorry. All I wanted to do is have fun in life, and I had fun when I was with you. Thank you for everything. Goodbye."

Finally, I was able to let go completely, and I felt at peace.

Later that night, I was surprised when the phone rang. "Is it alright if we talk?" Glenn asked.

It was the first time he had called me in months. My heart was pounding, but I calmly answered, "Sure," and we talked for several hours.

He said, "It was your statement about just wanting to have fun that made me think and want to call. Would you like to go on a ride to Sioux City for your birthday, strictly as friends?"

I could hardly contain my excitement and quickly said, "Yes," before he had a chance to change his mind.

On my birthday, he showed up on his Beemer. He looked genuinely happy to see me. I grabbed my helmet, jumped on the back of the bike, and off we went. He was very loving and attentive, much more than a friend ought to be. He laughed and talked with me, resting his hand on my knee the entire ride up. I was truly enjoying myself and the attention I was receiving.

We visited his friend, Todd, in Sioux City, Iowa. We were enjoying a movie and talking together, when Todd blurted out, "So, when are the two of you getting married?"

We just looked at each other, and I finally said to Glenn, "You've got to tell him."

So, Glenn confessed to Todd, "We are just friends, and we are currently broken up."

Todd quickly jumped to his feet and replied, "Glenn, I want to talk to you outside, *now.*" Glenn let out a sigh, but followed him grudgingly to the garage. They were gone for a long time.

Finally, someone is going to talk some sense into him!

Todd knew that we loved each other; he could see it for himself. He had told Glenn, "When you find someone who truly loves you, you shouldn't let them go."

Later that evening, Glenn took me out to eat for my birthday dinner. He was very warm and loving to me through dinner, and then he softly kissed my temple on the way out of the restaurant. *I know he wants me back.* The ride home on the motorcycle was very cold, so I had to snuggle up to him to keep warm. Glenn didn't seem to mind at all.

Two weeks dragged by until Glenn called and wanted to see me again. This time, it was me who was being leery. I told him, "I really need someone who is going to pay attention to me, wants to see me, and calls me more than once a week. I don't want to be just a girlfriend of convenience. I think that if we are to continue our relationship, we should talk to the pastor."

Glenn was reluctant to go because he knew that the pastor was rooting for our relationship. He would have preferred talking with someone who was more on his side. But he finally agreed to go. I quickly set up a meeting for the end of September with the pastor.

Pastor Tim told Glenn, "You cannot continue to be buddies. It is not right to keep leading her on. A decision has to be made either to let her go completely, or marry her. You need to set a time limit on your decision." We decided that a choice had to be made by April 6, which would be two years of dating. Pastor then told him, "I can guarantee that God will whisk her away and give her to someone who will love her. Now go home, get on your knees, and pray for God's will in this relationship, not yours. Surrender it completely to Him." Pastor Tim was such a wise man.

Glenn was a bit miffed when we left. That was not what he wanted to hear. I was thankful for the pastor's boldness. Maybe there would finally be a conclusion to this mess.

We did not see each other while Glenn was to be praying and listening for God's answer. At first, he refused to do it. He was afraid of what God would tell him. It was an agonizing time for me, but I continued to pray that God's will be done. I didn't want to make someone miserable again. I chose to follow the saying, "If you love something, set it free. If it comes

131

back to you, it's yours; if it doesn't, it never was." I loved Glenn very much, but I was willing to let him go if that was God's will for us.

Glenn eventually succumbed. He dropped to his knees and prayed, "Lord, I am asking for your will, and not my own, regarding Lori. I am so afraid of making another mistake. Please grant me wisdom and guidance as to what to do. In Jesus name, I pray. Amen." He continued to say this prayer for several days.

Three excruciating weeks had passed when Glenn finally called, "I would like to come by and talk to you." I was trying to read from the tone of his voice what his answer was, but he wasn't giving that away just yet. When he arrived, he said, "I feel differently about you, and I want to be with you." I could see a huge difference in him. The wall was coming down. He was beginning to allow me into his world, even though he was still afraid. I was overcome with relief.

He slowly became more attentive. He called more and wanted to see me more often. In time, he even got those three impossible words out of his mouth, "I love you." Not just "I love you," but "I really love you." I could genuinely feel that he loved me. I finally felt wanted and of value.

God was faithful! He had broken down the fortress that Glenn had surrounded himself with. God was not going to do this until both of us had surrendered everything, got out of His way, and let Him work.

Our love deepened with each passing week. We were shopping at Wal-Mart one day and came upon a rack of gaudy toe rings, which were $8 each. I tried on one with a heart-shaped stone. He said, "That would make a nice engagement ring."

I acted like I hadn't heard his comment, but my heart was racing when I placed the ring back on the rack.

The next night, he took me to a nice, but crowded, restaurant. He acted strange all evening, very distracted and non-communicative. When we left, he said, "How do you ask someone to marry you?"

That's what was going on tonight? "You just ask," I managed to say.

He confessed, "I was going to propose in the restaurant, but waiters kept coming over and there were too many people around. I also didn't have a ring to propose with."

I replied, "I would be perfectly happy with the ring I tried on at Wal-Mart to start with."

He scoffed and said, "I couldn't possibly be that cheap!"

I laughed and said, "It would just be temporary, and in the mean time, I will have something on my finger to be officially engaged."

We said goodnight, and I went home. I could barely sleep I was so incredibly happy. *He wants to marry me! Thank you, God!*

The following day was Sunday, December 21. We met at church since we lived in separate towns. He was late as usual and again acting odd. After church, everyone was standing around talking.

All of a sudden, he dropped down on one knee, took my hand, slipped the Wal-Mart toe ring on my finger, and asked, "Will you marry me?"

It didn't take me long to tell him, "Yes!"

"Don't you need time to think about it?"

"I've thought of nothing else for months," I replied.

"I'm just glad that you quit chasing me, so that I could catch you," he said with a smile.

I looked down at the beautiful ring on my finger and couldn't believe what was happening.

He relayed the rest of the story about the ring. "I went back to Wal-Mart this morning and searched through every ring to find the one that you had picked out. I was late because I couldn't find it. I finally found it, and went up to pay for it, and the ring was now on sale!"

I got so many compliments on what a beautiful ring it was and how expensive it looked. Everyone was shocked when we told them that it was not a $600 ring, but $6. Our friend Jim kidded, "We knew you were cheap, but we didn't think that you were that cheap!"

I couldn't stop looking at my ring. *I'm getting married!!*

Our friends Jim and Kathy started a Christian Motorcyclist Association (CMA) chapter in our area. Glenn and I wanted to serve the Lord together, and this seemed like a fantastic way to reach out to other bikers with the good news of Jesus Christ. We each chose a ministry that interested us. I chose the prison ministry because of Bob, and I hoped to identify with some of the struggles of the inmates. Glenn chose the servant's ministry since he was always helping others. It was wonderful to have a common bond. I felt that our union was going in a positive direction.

We started making wedding plans and decided on June 12, 2004, for the date. Neither of us wanted to go into debt with a wedding, so we made very simple plans and did a lot of bargain shopping. Thankfully, I already had the dress! In the course of six months, everyone was fully attired from items found at thrift stores. Everything was coming together nicely. I also found a heart-shaped, purple necklace to go with my dress.

Even though I loved my toe ring, the stones were starting to turn cloudy so we headed to the mall. After much debate, we chose a simple ring for me. For Glenn, we decided on a unique ring with three interlocking bands: one yellow, one white, and one of rose gold, which reminded us of Jesus's crown of thorns.

A month later, I received a jury summons for District court in the mail. It read, "Please report for jury duty on June 14." With despair, I screamed, "This can't be happening to me! I'm leaving on my honeymoon that day." I wrote a desperate letter to the judge explaining my dilemma. The judge's office called me back saying, "Due to the circumstances, you are granted two months off. Please report again in August."

Deciding on a honeymoon spot was another quandary. Glenn longed to see Alaska. I wanted to go to Arkansas to show him where I had gone with my mother. "Arkansas is definitely not my first choice, but we can go there if that's really what you want," he said.

"Well then, Arkansas it is!"

EIGHTEEN

Here comes the bride!

The Lord your God will fight for you, you need only to be still.
—Ex 14:14

June 12 finally arrived. It started out to be a sunny, calm day. *Thank you, God, for giving me such a lovely wedding day.* I couldn't wait to be married to Glenn.

Braden didn't feel that I had waited long enough after his father's death to start dating, so he chose not to attend the wedding. I tried to explain to him that I had been alone long before that, but I wasn't going to push him.

Instead of a flower girl, we chose an old-time custom of having a bell ringer start the ceremony. The wedding guests turned to listen to the gentle ringing of the bell. Three candles burned for our parents, who would be there with us in spirit.

Jamen looked quite handsome in his suit as he timidly entered my dressing room. From behind his back, he produced a small white box.

"I have been saving my money from work to buy you something special for your wedding day." My heart melted as I opened the box and beheld a beautiful "past, present, and future" pearl necklace. "I thought it would be perfect with your wedding dress," he said.

I stupidly said, "I have this purple necklace that I was going to wear."

"I understand," he replied, as he left us to finish dressing.

How could I be such an idiot? Stupid fool! I quickly switched necklaces, giving the purple one to my sister, Dina, who was my maid of honor. Jamen's gift went perfectly with my dress. He beamed with pride when I walked out of the room with it draped around my neck.

I took his arm as he escorted me down the aisle and handed me over to Glenn. Glenn's son, Tim, served as best man. I was terribly nervous and could barely utter my vows. The pastor introduced us as man and wife, and the song "Walk on Faith" began to play. Glenn whirled me around, and we danced down the aisle. It was so surreal!

At 6:00 P.M., an ominous bank of dark clouds rolled in. By the time that the reception started, there were severe thunderstorm warnings issued. By 10:00 P.M., the storms turned into tornado watches, and the guests decided to call it a night. Even with that, it was a very nice reception and the final cost for the evening was just under $900. Not bad for feeding 200 guests.

Tim and Jamen signed our wedding certificate. It was really special to have both of our sons as witnesses.

Jamen gave me a big hug as he was leaving. "I love you, Mom."

"I love you, too, Jarmie. You be really careful, will you?"

"I will. I promise. Bye, Mom. Have fun on your honeymoon."

Everything would be different from now on.

The following morning, I woke up beside my husband. I was with the man that I loved, and had never felt so safe and secure. *I was home!*

We left for Arkansas with absolutely no plans. "I am so tired of planning. Let's just pick a destination point and whatever we see in between will be a bonus," I said.

"I like that idea," Glenn replied.

"It will be a wonderful, relaxed, no-pressure honeymoon," I said.

The first night, we got a hotel room in Joplin, Missouri. After studying the room choices, Glenn picked out room number 208.

"It's right by a stairway door. Won't that be rather noisy?" I said.

"Well, then you pick a room," he replied.

The hotel clerk showed me a map of available rooms.

"Number 804 looks much quieter. We'll take this one," I said.

When we got outside, we could see where our room was: right over the office and very well lit. We then walked over to look at where room 208 was. "It doesn't have the noisy stairway door that I thought it had. You were right. Yours was a much better choice. Let's ask if we can switch back."

After explaining the situation, the clerk kindly obliged. We went to our room, and dead-bolted the door.

Bang! Bang! Bang! "Open up in there! This is the manager," a man yelled.

We both sat upright out of a dead sleep at about 2:00 A.M. "The night manager is trying to break our door down!" Glenn said.

"Get out of there, you squatters!" he screamed, while continuing to beat on the door.

"He's going to make it through the door as hard as he's kicking it," Glenn whispered.

Glenn yelled back, "We changed rooms. Go check room number 804 to verify it."

The manager stomped off muttering, "We'll just see about that."

We sat there stunned. About 10 minutes later, our phone rang. "This is the manager. I'm very sorry about all of this. The clerk showed me the error. I really apologize."

"It's alright. We are partly to blame for changing rooms," Glenn replied.

"If you come down to the lobby in the morning, we will give you a voucher for a free night in any same hotel." Glenn didn't feel right about accepting it, but I sure did. We checked out the next morning and picked up our free voucher.

The next day, we continued on our trip to Arkansas. I loved the area when I had been there before, and now I had the pleasure of sharing it with my new husband.

We went to the same Hoe Down that my mother and I had been to. I was pleased when Glenn said, "These guys are great! I am really having a wonderful time."

A block away from the Hoe Down, we found the same hotel chain as the one in Joplin. We showed the manager our voucher and asked, "Will you honor this?"

"With that voucher, you can have any room in the hotel," he replied.

"We'll take the honeymoon suite then, since we just got married a few days ago." He led us to a fantastic room that overlooked the forest. I could have happily stayed there forever.

Over the next few days, we stopped at a sunken steamship that had been found buried in a cornfield, complete with all of its cargo, as well as a Civil War woolen mill. I saw on the map that we were very close to the world's second-largest steam shovel, which was sixteen stories tall. I had been there before and knew that Glenn would love it. We drove the few miles over to Kansas, and standing before us was Big Brutus. Glenn was amazed by the sheer size of it. He admitted to me, "This is definitely the best vacation I've ever had." I had to agree.

After a week of play, it was time to get back home to start our new life together. Our first project was moving my things into Glenn's house. I left most everything for Braden since he would remain living in the trailer. So, moving mainly consisted of clothes and a few essentials.

August arrived, and the jury summons came as promised. I reported in and was chosen along with forty prospective jurors. In the courtroom, twenty-four of us were selected to possibly sit in on the trial, which was a child abuse case. Judge Ensz was presiding over the case. It was interesting to see how gentle and compassionate he really was. Judge Ensz told us about the case, and asked, "Have any of you had any dealings with child abuse before?"

I stood up, "I have, your Honor," and briefly told my story. Continuing, I said, "You were the judge that presided over Bob's case." The lawyers didn't feel that I would be an unbiased juror, so I was excused.

NINETEEN

Jamen

Train up a child in the way he should go, and when he is old,
he will not depart from it.

—Proverbs 22:6

One sunny September day, Jamen was driving me to town when I noticed
a photograph of his dad on the dash. "What's with the picture of your
dad?" I asked.

He replied, "It's a reminder to me of the type of person that I never
want to become." That comment struck me, but at the same time, I could
very much understand and was pleased to hear that he wanted something
better for his life. The chain can be broken.

Jamen graduated from high school in May of 2004 and turned eighteen
that same month. After graduation, he decided that he wanted to get as
far away from Nebraska as possible. "I want to go out west to Washington
or Oregon. I plan on being gone for two years. But I'll wait for you to get
married before I leave," he said.

"What will you do to survive for two years?" I asked.

"I plan on knocking on doors and asking people if they need help
along the way," he answered honestly.

Yikes! That sounds like a scary plan. So I offered, "Why don't you attend
the community college here?"

"College is not really on my list of things to do, Mom."

"The world out there is nothing like the safety that you have known
here, Jamen. You could really be putting yourself in danger," I cautioned.

"Alright, I won't knock on doors, but I will find something. I'll be
fine, Mom. Don't worry about me."

Don't worry? How can I not worry?

He was packed and ready to leave the morning after our wedding. I prayed, *Lord, I have to trust you to watch over him. He is totally out of my hands now. I'm giving him to You to watch over and keep safe.*

Our prayer group prayed specifically, *Lord guide him to where you want him to be. Grant him safety, direction, and give him a purpose.*

On June 13, Jamen headed north. I was going on my honeymoon and heading in the opposite direction. I jotted down two phone numbers and handed him the paper saying, "Here are Glenn's cell phone number and Philip's number in case you run into any problems."

On June 20, Jamen called. "I'm in Yellowstone National Park. It's no fun being on a trip alone. I'm having a miserable time, so I'm coming home."

I was so relieved! He told me, "On my way to Yellowstone, I heard an advertisement for a great hands-on college in computer technology. Can we call them?" We had been praying for direction and maybe this was where he was supposed to be. I called them and looked over the brochures that they sent. It sounded perfect for him. The one drawback was that it was in Rapid City, South Dakota, which was eight hours away from where we lived. Still, we decided to check it out.

Glenn, Jamen, and I drove up the next week to check out the college. Western Dakota Tech was a very small college with lots of one-on-one attention. We were all impressed with the staff and the school. The resident dorm manager gave us a tour and said, "I am a Christian, and I run a tight ship. No drugs, alcohol, or smoking are permitted." I was put more at ease as we continued to talk.

Everywhere I turned, I had confirmation that this was the right place for him. We returned home with the feeling that this was a real answer to prayer and where God wanted Jamen to be.

Jamen had been back from his adventure for two weeks when the cell phone rang. "Mom, I just had a car accident! I'm fine except for a cut finger, but the van is upside down in the ditch." My heart was racing. *Thank you, God, for protecting my baby!* Glenn and I drove there as fast as we could.

My heart sank when I saw the damage. The fenders, hood, and top of the van were completely smashed in. The front windshield was hopelessly shattered. "I can't believe that he escaped all of this with only an abrasion to his finger. He could have so easily been killed," I exclaimed.

Jamen hated seat belts but had worn one that day. He explained, "I was driving slowly down the gravel road. Since it had just rained, it was mushy on the sides and sucked me right into the ditch. I tried to over-correct. When I slammed on the brakes, it flipped me."

"Driving slowly, huh?" I said, not convinced. But once again, I thanked God for watching over him. It was a miracle that he was not badly hurt. God did not promise us that our lives would be trouble free, but He did promise to stand by us through each disaster. I was so thankful that He was along for the ride that day.

"Well, we have two weeks to find something reliable to get you to college. We have to use part of your college money, so we need to choose carefully," I told Jamen. I started to pray for the right vehicle.

Jamen excitedly called one day, "Mom, I found a 1989 Dodge van in great condition with low miles. I've already taken it out for a test drive. The car dealer told me that the original price was $4985, but they were going to give me a special price of just $2999! Hurry, Mom, you have to come see it before somebody else buys it!"

I said, "Slow down, let's check into this a little further."

That was not what he wanted to hear. Instead, I looked it up in the Kelly Blue Book, and saw that its true value was around $2400 in excellent condition.

Glenn and I went to the car lot and test-drove it the following day. The dealer told me about the amazing price that he had offered Jamen the day before. I responded, "Yes, I heard about it, but that price is still $500 over book." He didn't offer to come down, so we got up to leave. "Here is my email address in case you change your mind," I said.

The dealer emailed us several times in the next few days, saying, "We really would like your business." I emailed him back with the offer of $2400. Two days later, he wrote back, "We accept your offer."

Glenn said, "You really should have offered them $2000, or lower, due to the tires being worn out, the stereo not working, and other minor parts that needed replacing."

Again I prayed about it. *Lord, if this truly is the right vehicle, I pray that they would accept $2000 for it.*

Jamen was growing increasingly aggravated and ranted, "Why didn't you just give them the $2400?"

I replied, "We have to trust God on this one. If it's meant to be yours, we will get it. If not, then it wasn't the van we were supposed to buy."

I purposely waited a few days and emailed the dealer once again, "I'm sorry. I made an error in my first estimation. Attached is a list of all the items that need to be repaired. I am willing to come down today, with a check in hand for $2000, if that is acceptable to you." I was surprised when he wrote back and accepted my offer.

When we went to pick up the van, the salesman said, "I compliment you on your ability to deal."

Philip's graduation gift to Jamen was an expensive Gary Fisher mountain bike. A month after Jamen was at school, his new bike was stolen. He was so trusting of people, but I knew better and had written down the serial number and identifying information before he left. Taking the information, Jamen went to the police department and filed a theft report. "Sorry, nothing has been turned in matching that description. We will notify you if it's found," the officer told him.

I prayed daily, *Lord, you know who took Jamen's bike and where it is at this precise moment. I am asking that his bike be returned and in the condition that it was taken.*

Eight months passed and Jamen had come home for the summer with still no word about the bike. Deciding that it was not God's will to have the bike returned, I quit praying.

On June 17, 2005, I received a letter from the Rapid City Police Department. I ripped it open and read the words, "We have located your Gary Fisher bicycle and have it in our possession." *Thank you God!* The letter went on, "Please contact this office within fifteen days of receipt of this letter."

I rushed to the phone and called right away. The evidence clerk told me, "I'm sorry, but that bike was sold at auction because no one responded within the allotted time."

I explained to her, "I don't understand. The letter just arrived today." Then I saw that the letter was dated May 16. They had mailed it a month earlier to his dorm address, and it was finally forwarded to me. My heart sank. We had been so close.

She told me, "I will go and check the evidence room again and give you a call back." She didn't call.

I don't believe it, Lord! I refuse to believe that You would locate the bike for us, only to dangle it in front of us and take it away again. You are not that kind of God! Please may it be found, hidden in some dark corner?

I begged Glenn, "Please call the police department on Monday, and maybe you can find something out. They would have to have record of who bought it." Glenn called on Monday and spoke to a man this time.

The clerk looked in the computer and told Glenn, "The bike must have sold at auction on Saturday, because it no longer shows in the system."

"No! It's not possible, since I called and claimed it on Friday!" I replied in frustration.

The clerk called back a few hours later, "We have located your bike. They pulled it from the auction block on Friday and set it off in the corner. I'm sorry that you weren't notified."

I can't believe that we were within hours of losing that bike, and it was in good condition, just like I had prayed for. *Thank you, Lord for your goodness and mercy on us!*

Raising children is very hard, especially when they are nineteen and no longer feel that they have to abide by what you say. I spent so much of my time trying to protect them from mistakes and failures that I had in turn done them an injustice. Our pastor told us, "Pray for your kids. Turn them over to God. Let them make their mistakes, and stay out of it!" I think that is the hardest thing in the world for a parent to do. I did my children no favors by trying to make everything better. It made them ill-equipped to handle the cruel world. I wanted to shield and protect them, but they have to fall, make mistakes, and learn just like I did. That is the only way that they will grow.

Jamen graduated from college on May 13, 2006, with an associate's degree in electronic technology. I had chosen not to go to the graduation, somewhat for practical reasons, but also for selfish ones. I tried to justify it in my mind. *It's an eight-hour drive one way at $2.90-a-gallon gas. He won't really mind; most kids don't even attend their college graduation.*

I told him, "I will give you the money that I would have used for the trip for your graduation present instead. Is that alright with you?" I wrote to him several times, "Are you sure it's okay with you that I miss graduation?" He never gave me an answer. I had the nagging feeling that I was making the wrong choice.

He called me the night of graduation crying, "All of my friends came to my graduation, and you weren't here!"

All I could do was tell him, "I'm so sorry, Jarmie. I didn't realize how much it meant to you. I'm really sorry!" *I'm the worst mother that's ever lived.* I had hurt my son deeply. I spent the next several hours mentally beating myself up and then realized, *I can't undo what I've done. He didn't want my money. He wanted me, and I let him down.*

I confessed my failures to my friend, Carrie, who replied, "You know those boys still need love and affection, but they just don't want to admit it. Just remember that God is bigger than all of our failures; give it to Him and let go of it. Don't let Satan make you feel so guilty and ashamed. He loves to steal our joy and render us ineffective. Remember, God is in control of every detail of our life and working everything out for our good."

I wrote to Jamen and told him how terribly sorry I was that I had hurt him. Thankfully, he wrote back and said, "I was really hurt, Mom, but I forgive you." And so I picked myself up and moved on, trying not to repeat my failures again.

When the boys were young, I prayed specifically for whom they would marry someday. Jamen married a girl who truly complements him, named Julie Walker. The wedding was held in Wyoming on June 27, 2009.

Julie was one of my editors for this book. After she finished reading it, she told me, "Oh, my goodness! Jamen has never told me any of this in the three years that we have been together!"

I replied, "It's probably good that you know, since the past can't stay buried forever. Before the pastor married them, he told Jamen, "I want you to read your mother's manuscript. I think there are unresolved issues that need to be dealt with." Jamen refused. He isn't ready to relive the pain just yet.

The circle of life continued on December 5, 2010, when Cooper Tyler Lang entered the world, and I began the new role of Grandma. I was so relieved that Cooper didn't arrive on December 7, the 10th anniversary of Bob's death.

Bob's mother was thrilled to become a great-grandmother for the first time. But Bob has missed so much of his sons' lives, graduations, weddings, and now the birth of his grandson. Cooper will also never have the chance to get to know his grandpa.

At five months old, Cooper contracted Respiratory Syncytial Virus (RSV). Fighting for his life, he was quickly hospitalized and placed on oxygen. *Please, God, please don't take him! Jamen can't handle another loss. Please spare his life. Please, Lord, I'm begging you. Don't take him.* I wept uncontrollably for days. My boss stopped what he was doing, approached my desk, and prayed with me. That really touched my heart. Cooper was released from the hospital several days later, still a sick little boy, but he was going to make it. *Thank you, Jesus!*

TWENTY

Ministry opportunities

*For this very reason I have raised you up, that I may show my power
in you, and that My name may be declared in all the earth.*
—Romans 9:17

I had completed the Christian Motorcyclist Association prison ministry course, but had not done anything with it, so I called the juvenile detention center in Madison. "Several of our members would like to come in each month and share our testimony with the kids." They were very accommodating and eager for us to come. If just one child's life could be changed by our testimony, it would be well worth it. I felt like I could genuinely identify with what many of these children were going through. The jail where Bob was incarcerated sat adjacent to the detention center, and I knew it would again be an emotional time.

We had our first opportunity to get our feet wet by witnessing to a youth group. I relayed the stories about losing my mom, being rejected by my dad, and being abused by my husband. I told them, "People are going to let you down in this life. But we have a God who will never let you down. Hebrews 13:5 says: 'I will never leave you, nor forsake you.'" I was so pleased that God was able to use someone like me.

One cold December night, the director from the detention center called, "Could you come in tonight and visit with a girl who tried to commit suicide last night? She feels that no one loves or cares for her. Maybe you can get through to her."

"I'll be there right away," I replied.

This girl was not allowed visitors, but God opened up that door to me since I had dealt with suicide previously. I spent two hours with her, and before I left, she prayed to accept Christ into her heart. We have a heavenly Father who longs to be with us and wants only the best for us. God will use our trials at some point in time if we allow Him to.

One day, we were invited to a birthday dinner at a restaurant in York, Nebraska, with CMA friends. We decided to ride our bikes down and wear our leathers. After the meal, Glenn went into the restroom and washed his hands. An inebriated man came up behind him and started reading the verse that was on the back of Glenn's jacket. It read: "For God so loved the world, that He gave his only begotten Son, that whosoever believeth in Him, should not perish but have everlasting life." (John 3:16)

The man scoffed, "God could never love a drunk like me."

Glenn quickly replied, "God does love you! That is exactly why He sent His son to die, for you." Glenn shared more about God's love with this man. This stranger then prayed with Glenn right there in that bathroom to accept Jesus into his life. He came and sat with us at the birthday celebration, and what a celebration it was! Luke 15:7 says: "When one sinner repents, the angels rejoice!"

I have a friend who once asked me, "How and why do you choose to dredge up everything over and over? I was abused, and I just want to bury it all and never think about it again."

I asked her, "But what good is all of that buried knowledge doing for someone else who is hurting? If I can help one person to heal, then it is worth reliving the pain because I know that God wants to set them free."

I finally had purpose in my life!

Three months before Glenn's dad passed away, we stopped for a visit. Glenn wanted one more opportunity to share Jesus with his dad. John was ninety years old, and Glenn was afraid that his dad would pass from this life not knowing for certain that he would be going to heaven. Glenn asked, "Dad, do you know where you will spend eternity?"

His dad shrugged his shoulders. "I don't know," he replied.

I ran out to the car to grab my Bible and handed it to Glenn. He told his dad, "Jesus came to seek and save those who were lost, which is all of us. He died on the cross to cover all of your sins, but it is a free gift that each man must decide to accept or reject. Romans 10:13 says: 'For whosoever calls on the name of the Lord shall be saved.' Would you like to pray with me to receive Christ, Dad?"

John nodded that he would, and the two of them prayed together. "Father, please forgive me of my sins. I believe that You died on the cross for me, and I ask You to come into my life and save me. Thank You for giving Your life as a ransom for mine. Amen." Glenn then asked his dad again, "Where will you spend eternity, Dad?"

"I'll be in heaven!" he said with a radiant smile.

"Yes, you will!" Glenn joyfully replied.

Glenn cried the entire way home, having the assurance that he would see his dad in heaven one day.

His dad closed his eyes on this earth and opened them in heaven just three months later.

Kathy and I have been approved to minister to the ladies incarcerated at the Nebraska Correctional Center for Women in York. So begins a new journey for us.

TWENTY ONE

Jim's Vision

Therefore, if anyone is in Christ, he is a new creation; old things
have passed away; behold all things have become new.
—II Corinthians 5:17

Friends are so important to each of us, reflecting who we are and, often, how we grow mentally and spiritually. God uses others to speak into our lives. Through our friendships, we can learn to love and trust, despite our circumstances.

In September 2007, our dear friend, Jim, lost his courageous fight with cancer. Days before he passed away, Jim and Kathy had settled down for the night, but she couldn't sleep. She fervently prayed, "God, why haven't You answered my prayers to heal Jim?"

Suddenly Jim called out, "Kathy, are you awake?"

"Yes," she replied," I'm awake."

Jim said, "We are in a room, with people standing all around us. Some of the people in the room I know. I see Glenn and Lori. Kathy, are you awake?"

"Yes, Jim," she said with more urgency. "I am fully wide awake!"

Jim whispered, "There is someone coming who's taller than all the rest of us."

"Who is it?" Kathy inquired.

"It's Jesus!" he replied.

"What's happening now?" Kathy asked, wishing that she could see into his vision.

"He's coming toward us and standing near the water. Someone is going toward him carrying a belt."

"What is the belt?" Kathy asked.

"It's the belt of sin, and they are laying it at His feet," Jim said.

"Kathy, He's looking at me!" he exclaimed.

"Why is He looking at you?" Kathy asked.

"I'm supposed to do something," Jim replied.

"Well, what is it?"

"I'm not sure, but there is a paper bag with shoes and clothes in it. I think I'm supposed to take the bag and give it to Him."

"Then do it, Jim," Kathy said. And the vision was gone.

What a wonderful gift was this vision. Glenn and I were thrilled to hear that we were there! And we were sure to point that part out to all those listening to the story, which made Jim smile. Later, we found out that a friend of ours named Donna had accepted Christ into her heart that same night. We wondered if this was the same person that Jim saw handing over the belt to Jesus.

Glenn tried to explain the part about the shoes and paper bag. "When we were children and would go to someone's house for the night, we would put all of our clothes and shoes in a paper bag. It was our traveling bag, in lieu of a suitcase. I believe that is what Jesus wanted for Jim to bring along, for his 'trip.' The belt, I am assuming, is the sin that we all carry around. Jesus took Donna's sin when she handed it over to Him."

Jim was in the hospital, surrounded by his family, when he went home to be with the Lord. Kathy said, "We weren't afraid but felt totally at peace." Jim didn't want to leave his family, but Kathy told him, "Its okay for you to go, Jim."

We know that God welcomed him home with open arms that day saying, "Well done, good and faithful servant."

Jim's going home celebration was a true testimony of his life, which was to spread the good news that Christ died for each person there. Jim had touched so many lives. He told us when he left California as a younger man, only one person said goodbye because of the rough life that he had led while there. He would have been thrilled to see over four hundred people at his funeral, all because of the change Jesus made to his life.

Over one hundred motorcycles, each carrying an American flag, and being led by two riders with the CMA flag and American flag, escorted him to his final resting place. Kathy rode on Jim's bike, driven by their friend, Ed. Never before have I seen so much leather at a funeral. Full military rites were given at the cemetery. It was a fitting farewell to a wonderful husband, father, friend, defender of our country, and beloved child of God.

Kathy is bravely going on, leaning on God each day for strength. She has decided to go on with the prison ministry and to speak for Jim, telling his story.

TWENTY TWO

The Best Valentine!

*Greater love has no one than this, than to lay down one's life
for his friends.*

—John 15:13

Valentine's Day of 2007 was unique. Four months prior, I had broken a bone in my foot while chopping weeds in the pasture. Moles were industriously digging holes, which I happened to step in. Each time, I went to the doctor he would tell me the same discouraging news, "I'm sorry, but it's not healing. Stay completely off of it and come back in a month." My foot was horribly swollen and colored deep shades of purple. Glenn was afraid that I might lose my foot.

He excitedly called me at work one day and said, "Leeches! What about using leeches? They are supposed to recycle the blood and have eliminated amputations in some cases."

I was willing to try anything at this point, so I agreed.

A friend told him, "There is a creek near our farm that contains leeches. Feel free to go out and get as many as you need."

On Valentine's Day, Glenn grabbed his bucket and headed to the creek. He rolled up his pant legs, and removed his shoes and socks before heading into the icy water. He gathered up as many leeches as he could into the container, before his feet went numb in the frigid stream. Greater love hath no man for his wife than this.

When he arrived home with the bucket of nasty, slimy creatures, he sat me on the couch and propped my foot on the coffee table. I promptly pulled a blanket over my head so that I wouldn't have to watch as he placed them one by one onto my swollen foot. He waited with anticipation for them to attach. The fat black worms tickled my foot as they slithered around, trying to find an acceptable place to suck on.

"It's so disgusting!" I screamed.

With many failed attempts to get them to attach, and following all the directions to the letter that we had found on the Internet, we came to the sad realization that these were algae eaters and not blood suckers.

Surgery was scheduled to pin the bones back together in case the last x-ray showed no signs of healing. A prayer request was sent out, asking people to pray that it had healed enough to avoid the surgery. When I went in the following day for my appointment, I was so thrilled to hear that God had answered our prayers and that the bone was finally starting to heal. Five months after the injury, I was finally able to put a little weight on my foot. When I was able to use it again, the swelling and discoloration went away. Glenn was ecstatic when I could walk again. He had been keeping the house running for all those months.

Glenn had taken flying lessons in 1978 but wasn't able to complete the course due to being laid off at work. It had been his dream to finish what he had begun. On Valentine's Day 2010, I made arrangements for him to have two hours of flying instructions. I made a card that read, "This entitles you to two hours of flying at the Columbus (Nebraska) airport. Live out your dream, Baby!" He must have read the card five times to grasp the realization of what it read.

He quickly made the appointment with the instructor before I changed my mind. Small engine planes have always been a fear of mine. I have heard of too many plane crashes to feel comfortable with them.

His sister, Millie, and I went along the following week to photograph this memorable moment. With great anticipation, Glenn grabbed the controls of the plane and taxied away. We watched as the little plane soared into the cloudless sky.

All the way home, he replayed the experience in his mind, saying, "That was so awesome! I can't wait to go up again! I love you so much!"

He later told me, "I heard about a ministry where pilots deliver pastors to remote areas in foreign countries. Maybe that is where God will lead us someday."

"Yes, we can both die in a jungle plane crash," I sarcastically remarked.

It's wonderful that Braden and Glenn have so much in common. I think God predestined that long ago, so that there would be a connection between the two.

When Braden was thirteen, he was already 6'3" and seemed older than he was. I read in the newspaper that the airport was having a special deal, where you could take a flight lesson for $35. Braden loved airplanes and I thought it would be the perfect gift, so in August of 1997, we took the whole family to the Carl Steffen Memorial Airport in Norfolk.

It was a cloudless day and the winds were perfect for flying. When we arrived at the airport, they had a very small Cessna 150 waiting; it hardly looked like it could hold two people. Braden eagerly went to talk to the pilot, who gave him basic instructions before take-off.

As they taxied past us, Braden shot us a huge grin and waved goodbye. We all waved back as they slowly made their ascent into the sky. He flew around Norfolk with the instructor for 20 minutes. When it came time to land, the pilot took his hands off of the controls and allowed Braden to land the plane. Bob and I had such a feeling of pride as we watched the plane come in. Braden's face was fixed with total concentration as he taxied in.

He was so excited when he climbed out of the plane, telling us every detail of his experience, from take-off to landing. Bob suggested that we could get him lessons full time, and he could get his pilot license. He felt that he would be more apt to get a good job someday with that on his resume. It would be about $4000 to complete the hours needed. Bob said it would be an investment in Braden's future. It was a wonderful thought, but it never came to pass.

TWENTY THREE

Incarceration

But God demonstrates His own love toward us, in that while we were still sinners, Christ died for us.

—Romans 5:8

In November 2007, Bob's brother Peter was driving erratically, swerving all over the road. In the next lane, a woman was driving alongside him with her young son. She angrily yelled out her window, "You're going to kill somebody driving like that!" He proceeded to pull out a 9MM handgun and pointed it directly at her.

She quickly stopped and called the police, who arrived and placed him into custody. He was taken to the regional center for the mentally ill, where he continues to reside.

Peter had been a successful lawyer. I believe that Bob's suicide had something to do with his brother going off the deep end. It's amazing how our actions continue to affect those around us.

Braden didn't make it down to his grandparents' house for Christmas and had no idea that Peter was not there to look after Grandma. He drove down on New Year's Day, only to discover Grandma lying on the floor.

"Oh my gosh! Grandma, what happened?" he yelled, racing to her side.

"I'm okay. I'm so glad to see you! I didn't think anyone would ever come," she managed to say.

"Are you hurt? How long have you been lying here?"

"I fell six days ago. I think I broke my hip," she replied.

Braden quickly called the ambulance.

He turned his attention back to Grandma, "Where is Peter? Why isn't he taking care of you?"

"He was arrested a month ago," Grandma replied.

Temperatures dipped down to minus 1 that week. The front door was ajar, causing a considerable draft where she lay shivering. The heat from the furnace rose to the ceiling, leaving the floor penetratingly cold.

"I pulled myself over to a stack of newspapers and placed them over me to keep warm. I've been sharing my bottle of apple juice with the dog this past week," she confessed. "Someone came to the door a few days ago. I called out, but I guess he couldn't hear me." She looked around at the conditions she had been forced to live in, "I'm so sorry for all the mess."

"It's alright, Grandma. Don't worry about it. I'm just so glad that I found you in time," he replied.

The ambulance arrived and took her to the hospital where her broken hip was tended to.

Braden remained at the farm for several days, taking care of things in her absence. He visited her in the hospital every day. Bob's sister, Naomi, had been trying to call her mom for several days. She grew increasingly concerned when neither Peter nor Grandma would answer the phone and called the police to check on her, whom Grandma had heard come to the door earlier in the week. Unfortunately, the officer couldn't hear Grandma's faint cries for help and left.

Braden called Naomi and relayed the events of the previous week. Without hesitation, she drove from her home in Idaho. "You're going to come live with us, so that we can take care of you," she told Grandma.

"I don't want to leave the farm. This is my home," Grandma replied.

"Mom, you can't stay here alone again, and we don't know how long Peter will be gone. So, let's pack your things and be on our way." Grandma would never return to the farm, again, but found a new life in Idaho.

TWENTY FOUR

What Now?

Therefore do not throw away your confidence, which has a great reward. For you have need of endurance, so that when you have done the will of God you may receive what is promised.
—Hebrews 10:35-36

Glenn and I truly enjoy each other's company. There is so much laughter in our home. I have forgotten what it was like to live in fear, being controlled, manipulated, and criticized. I am blessed far beyond what I deserve. When I cry, Glenn cries with me.

He tells me daily, "I'm so glad that I married you. I love you so much!" For the first time, I am valued, prized, and respected. I also have a love for him that I didn't think was possible. I find myself wanting to do things for him. I make sure that he has a lunch packed and that I greet him at the door every day with a kiss. I am his helpmate when cutting firewood or working in the field. With Bob, I couldn't do anything right. Glenn makes me feel like I can't do anything wrong. It's strange how two men can see the same person so differently.

When there is a problem that arises between us, I can go to Glenn immediately and discuss it with him. I can tell him when I've been hurt by something that was said. With Bob, I never had that freedom. Bob didn't care how I felt. I kept so many things bottled up inside. I can go to Glenn right away to resolve any issues that stand between us, so that we can come together in unity again.

Glenn told me recently, "I was the one who had held onto my baggage for so long, burdens that I thought I had dealt with long ago, but I realize I never really had. I'm ready to truly forgive my ex-wife." He prayed to do just that, and knows in his heart that he has now completely forgiven her.

In the past, I tried to gain Bob's approval and acceptance, thinking that if I looked my best for him that he would be pleased with me. Glenn loves and accepts me no matter what. I can just be me, and that is so freeing.

With Bob, I dreaded coming home, always wondering what the night was going to be like, praying that I could be somewhere else. I now look forward to coming home; I can't wait to see Glenn at the end of the day.

Glenn is very protective of me. He worries about me when I am late from work, and especially when I am driving in the dark since I am night blind. On the highway, he put a reflector on the sign post so that I could see where to turn to come home. To me, that is true love.

Eight months after we were married, Glenn came home and said, "Today at work, I was told that I could either go to the night shift or take a lay off. I think I'm going to have to take the night shift."

"You've been there for nineteen years! How can they do this to you? I'll never see you," I cried.

"I'm sorry, Baby, I don't have much choice."

For the following months, I woke him up from a dead sleep to see him for five minutes every morning. It was hard to discuss anything of importance to someone half asleep. I told him, "Goodbye, I'll see you tomorrow. I love you!" The separation was very hard on us. I finally had a husband I truly wanted to be with, and now couldn't.

We made up a list of our wants and needs, and began praying on that list, asking for God's direction and guidance. Several months later, our situation was still the same. The thought crossed my mind to find a night-shift job for myself so that we could be together.

Lord, I believe that You put Glenn and I together so that we wouldn't be alone. Well, I'm sitting here alone, and I don't like it one bit. I recalled the story of Abraham and Sarah. They didn't wait for the Lord's answer but went off on their own, and it was disastrous for them. I had been through enough disasters, so I continued to pray and wait upon the Lord for His answer.

Glenn and I viewed our separation differently. "I think this is drawing us closer, because I miss you all the time," he said.

I retorted, "I have decided to invest in a sticky note company, as that is our sole means of communication. This separation is pulling us apart,

159

not drawing us closer. I've gotten used to being alone and doing things without you, and I don't like that. That is not why I got married."

"We still have our weekends together," he replied with an ornery smile.

"You are still on a different sleep schedule, so we really don't," I added with frustration.

On June 5, 2005, we attended the Nebraska State CMA rally. Roger, the regional evangelist, asked if anyone had a prayer request. Glenn and I went forward to be prayed over about his job situation. Five months had gone by and still there was no answer. Roger prayed such a powerful prayer over us, asking for a blessing on our marriage to hold it strong, binding Satan, and that God would turn this situation around. He will give you the desires of your heart, if you seek Him first—though sometimes I wish that these answers would come a little more quickly.

I wasn't looking for another job. I loved the people I worked with, but I didn't like the twenty two-mile commute each way in the winter. On July 25, 2005, my friend Kally told me about an administrative assistant's job in Madison. I filled out an application only to appease her, and sent it in. I didn't expect to hear back from them and didn't care if I did.

The following day I was called in for a job interview. I was impressed by everything and felt that God had brought me there. I left the interview satisfied and encouraged. When the phone rang at 9:00 P.M. that night, I thought it was Kally asking me how the interview went. Instead, it was the owner, "We would like to offer you the job if you're interested."

"I need to talk to my husband first, if that's alright. I will call you tomorrow with my answer."

Glenn was excited for me, "I would like to see you on the road less. Maybe this would give us a chance to at least have lunch together." I loved the thought of being able to spend more time with him. It made this job quite tempting.

The next day, all of my excitement had turned into doubt. I was terribly upset all day. *What if I'm making a horrible mistake?* After many agonizing hours, I heard a small voice in my head that said, "Trust Me." The door had clearly been opened to me, so I decided to take a blind leap of faith and accept the offer.

Kathy reminded me, "Look at all that you are gaining, and don't focus on what you're losing. Every extra moment with Glenn is time that you can't get back." God clearly had his hand in all of this. We had been so focused on asking for Glenn's job situation to turn around that I hadn't been praying about mine. However, God was always working on my behalf even when I wasn't asking.

I was so blessed to have wonderful Christian employers. There have been times when I have come to work with a problem, and they have stopped what they were doing and prayed with me to resolve it. That meant so much to me. I felt valued and appreciated, like that was clearly where I was supposed to be.

Glenn continued to apply for jobs. He was offered a night-shift position and told that, in two years, this could work into a first-shift position. We compared it to our prayer list and decided, "This isn't what we have been praying for." Glenn declined the offer, and we continued to wait.

That September, Millie handed him a posting of an upcoming first-shift position at B-D Medical in Columbus. Glenn applied immediately. Five weeks later, he was told that they were going to hire internally. Our hopes were dashed once again, but we continued to pray.

In October, we attended a CMA Rally in Hatfield, Arkansas. I was relishing an entire week with my husband. It was 36 frigid degrees when we left on the bike, and I was just about frozen to death by the time we stopped at a restaurant a few hours later.

The rally was amazing, with nearly four thousand leather-clad bikers raising their hands in worship to God. Glenn rarely left my side and I savored every moment, knowing it would soon come to an end.

Nine months had passed since we began praying for Glenn's job when we noticed the red light flashing on the phone. "This is B-D Medical. We were unable to fill the first-shift position internally. Would you still be interested?" Fear soon set in just as it had with me. He had been with his current company for most of his career, and a move now was terrifying.

"This could only have been from God," he rationalized. We compared the job to our prayer list and saw that He had answered our entire list of needs and wants. God was faithful, and Glenn accepted the job offer. I had my husband back to share my life with. "This is the best job that I have ever had," he said.

Glenn was asked by a coworker one day, "How did you get on first shift without doing your time on the night shift? No one walks in here on first shift."

"God opened this job for me," he replied assuredly.

TWENTY FIVE

A Time of Healing

*Now to Him who is able to do exceedingly abundantly above all
that we ask or think.*

—Ephesians 3:20

In December 2006, Braden graduated college with a Bachelor of Science in Biology. The boy, whose dad said he would never go to college, finished in the upper part of his class. "Daddy would have been so proud of you," I told him.

On May 10, 2008, Braden married the perfect girl for him by the name of Krista Eucken. She chose to wear my wedding dress and was a stunning bride. Both of the boys have chosen very well, for which I am quite pleased. The boys are fortunate to have wives who truly complete and complement them. The girls both possess integrity worthy of respect. To both of my daughters-in-law: "Many daughters have done well, but you excel them all." (Proverbs 31:28-29)

That year, Braden invited us over for Thanksgiving. Later that evening, he was sitting on the kitchen floor leaning against the wall and asked, "Do you think the fire is what drove Daddy to kill himself?" And so began several hours of discussion for the first time since Bob's death.

I replied, "The fire was probably part of it, but there were many extenuating circumstances that caused him to make that choice. He had lost everything and was a broken man at that point."

I continued, "I am so sorry that I let you down and failed to protect you." I tried to explain why I made the choices that I had, and for the first time since the fire, Braden hugged me back when we went to leave. I cried the whole way to the hotel. *Thank you, God, for this Thanksgiving of healing.*

In 2009, Braden announced, "I've decided to go into law enforcement like Daddy and Grandpa."

"But you went to school to be a biologist."

"I know, but there aren't any biology jobs, and if there is one, it's just seasonal. I have a wife to support now and need full-time work."

"Yes, I guess you do."

On a snowy December day, we attended the graduation ceremony at the Nebraska Law Enforcement Training Center. The auditorium was filled with excitement as everyone waited for the commencement to begin. My chest filled with pride as I watched him fall in line and take his place with the other graduates to repeat the oath.

After the ceremony, Braden proudly showed us around and led us to the prior class photos. He stopped at the class of 1978 and pointed out his dad's picture. Staring back at me was the man that I knew so long ago. And now his son would follow in his footsteps to uphold the law. Once again, his dad would have been proud of the fine, young man he has turned out to be.

I prayed so many times over my boys that the sins of the father would not be passed onto the next generation, but that our mistakes will end here and now with us. Ezekiel 18:20 gives me that hope by saying: "The soul who sins is the one who will die. The son will not share the guilt of the father, nor will the father share the guilt of the son. The righteousness of the righteous man will be credited to him, and the wickedness of the wicked will be charged against him."

At times, when I am alone, something will spark a memory of Bob. A twinge of guilt and regret surfaces once again. Memories of my dad's betrayal haunt me every so often. I brush away the pain and try to think of a happier time. I will most likely carry those memories the remainder of my life. I have made a conscious choice, though: *I won't allow these memories to destroy me.*

It's funny that some of the things about Bob that drove me crazy, like separating trash and using sun protection, are things I have adopted into my life. I can see the importance of it and have to admit that maybe he was right after all. Maybe it was just the child in me not wanting to be told what to do that caused me to rebel against his rules.

Bob's sister sent me a letter. I was a bit hesitant to open it, not knowing her feelings toward me, but the letter was warm and welcoming. I responded and told her what life had been like, but also that Bob might have accepted Christ before he died. She was pleased to hear that, and we have kept in touch, sharing the latest news about the boys and Cooper.

※

On a tombstone, there is a dash in between the date you are born and the date that you die. Our pastor asked us one Sunday, "What have you done with your dash?" In reflection, I wasted most of my dash on selfish desires. Now I am choosing to do something with that time by trying to give something back to God who has given me so much.

Even through all the chaos, God was in total control. He turned our tragedy around and brought good out of it. Having already seen my entire life in preview, He knew the part that everyone would play and what the outcome would be. None of this came as a surprise to Him. We have been blessed by wonderful friends, and a loving God who guided and protected us.

Even in all my confusion, when I was relying upon myself to get us out of each disaster, He was there. I am hoping that this book will in some way be able to help someone who is in a similar situation by offering hope. There is a God who loves you. Nothing is beyond His reach. "God is our refuge and strength, a very present help in times of trouble; therefore we will not fear even though the earth be moved." (Psalm 46)

Writing this has been a tremendous healing process for me. It has been an avenue to deal with, and release, the pain. I have a merciful God who has been right by my side and endured the pain with me. Psalms 34:17 says: "The Lord is near to those who have a broken heart." I truly believe that I am a stronger person today for having gone through these trials.

I was completely finished writing this book and had purposely left out the part about the abortion. I was incredibly ashamed. I was afraid of baring myself to face rejection, although I have wonderful friends who love me and who will forgive and support me. Everyone had been told that I had a miscarriage, and I was satisfied that the secret never had to be revealed. But I felt God tapping me on the shoulder saying, "You need to include that painful time. You have no idea how many women have gone through what you have. It's important that you tell them they are not alone."

I fought with God for quite a while on this. *No, God, please don't make me do this!* I pleaded. But He won in the end.

God is so faithful by sending people to encourage me. I allowed a friend of mine to read this manuscript. I was hoping she would take it home to read in private, but she sat right next to me and flipped it open, reading my biggest shame right in front of me. I shrank away inside, fearing the rejection. She finished reading that chapter, turned, and said warmly to me, "Oh Lori, that must have been so hard for you to write. God will surely use your pain to help other women who have gone through this. Thank you for being so brave to include this in your story." I was so relieved by her kind words. It reassured me that I had done the right thing to include that painful part of my life. I love God's little confirmations.

Thirty years have passed, and this is the first time that I have been able to talk about the abortion. I think that it would have be much easier to admit if I was an alcoholic or drug addict, than it is to admit that I was responsible for the death of my own child. I have felt so much guilt and shame for a selfish choice made that I wasn't even able to tell my closest friends about it. But I am reminded in Isaiah 1:18: "Though your sins are like scarlet, I will make them white as snow."

For Christmas 2010, I received a gift that brought me to tears. Glenn's son, Tim, gave me two copies of the book, *The Story of Ferdinand*. One copy was to replace Mama's that burned in our house fire. The other copy was for me to pass on to my grandson, Cooper. It never ceases to amaze me that God continues to replace what the locusts have eaten.

The Bible is full of promises. They are written for us to grab hold of to have hope. I am so grateful that God hand-picked me to be a part of all of this. Psalms 56:8 says: "He holds all of my tears in a bottle!" I have cried enough tears to fill an ocean.

What love He must have for me to want to hold onto all of my tears! It shows me that He doesn't want me to carry the pain any longer but wants me to give it all over to Him to hold. Isaiah 49:16 says: "See, I have inscribed you in the palms of My hands." I am so special to God that He carved my name into His hands where it cannot be erased or blotted out. What a comfort that is. God was definitely holding onto me when I didn't have the strength to hold onto Him.

The following are some Bible verses that have helped me through some of my darkest moments. God wants only the best for us and He is faithful. We only have to be willing to "Let go, and let God."

"Cast your burden on the Lord, and He shall sustain you." (Psalms 56:22)

"The righteous cry out and the Lord hears and delivers them out of all their troubles." (Psalms 34:17)

"Trust in the Lord with all your heart; lean not on your own understanding. In all your ways, acknowledge Him and He shall direct your paths." (Proverbs 3:5)

"Return to the Lord, your God, for He is gracious and merciful, slow to anger and of great kindness, and He relents from doing harm." (Joel 2:13)

If you would like to let go and let God begin the healing process, allow Him into your life by praying this prayer:

> *Lord Jesus, I am a sinner in need of Your salvation. I believe that You and God the Father are One, and that You paid my penalty on the cross, taking all of my sins upon Yourself. I now call upon Your name and ask You to save me. Thank you Jesus. Amen. (Romans 10:13)*

It's that simple, and He has assured you a place in heaven by doing so.

If you have trusted in Jesus as your savior, your salvation is secure. You have been adopted into God's family. Ephesians 2:19 says that you are now a member of the household of God! A seal was placed upon you by the Holy Spirit (Ephesians 1:13), and the only way to be separated from Christ would be to pry open God's hand and be snatched from the Son (John 10:28-29). The Bible says that there is joy in the presence of angels over one sinner who repents (Luke 15:10). I know that my mother was in heaven when I truly accepted Jesus into my heart and that she was one of those celebrating in the presence of angels over me. I can't wait to spend all of eternity with her.

This is something I believe should not be procrastinated about. As I have found out, you never know if tomorrow will come.

Jesus said, "I am the way, the truth and the life. No one comes to the father, but by me." (John 14:6) God did not send His Son into the world to condemn the world, but that the world through Him might be saved (John 3:17).

He is always there to guide, protect, and give you the strength to make it through another day. He cares for you and will go out of His way to rescue you when you call on Him concerning every problem that you face. What a comforting thought that is! I have called on Him often, and He has never failed to answer me. Sometimes it is not the answer that I expect, but it is always the way that He intends the outcome to be, and it will always turn out.

In Daniel 10:13, the archangel Michael was sent to help Daniel but was delayed twenty one days because he was battling a great demon, the Prince of Persia. I wondered how many times that God had sent an angel to help me that was delayed in an unseen battle.

As I am reading through this book and editing it for the hundredth time, I find that every time I read it, I sit here and cry. Many times, I can't see the keys to type, through all my tears. There has been so much pain and sorrow!

But by God's grace, I am A *SURVIVOR*!

ABOUT THE EDITOR

Rita Brhel is a freelance editor/writer from Fairfield, Nebraska, where she lives with her husband and three children on a small farm.

Rita was drawn to work on this book because of Lori's passion and compassion to reach out to others in similar circumstances. Rita has personal experience in supporting a loved one with bipolar disorder and is intimately aware of the difficulties that families go through when faced with the devastation of mental illness. Rita relies heavily on God for his guidance and grace and, through her work with this book, is encouraged to help empower others who may be struggling to support a loved one with mental illness.

Rita can be contacted by e-mail at rita.brhel@gmail.com or by writing: 807 East 4th Street, Fairfield, NE 68938.

Lori can be contacted by e-mail at cheney78@hotmail.com